IMMIGRATION AND FAITH

IMMIGRATION AND FAITH

CULTURAL, BIBLICAL, AND THEOLOGICAL NARRATIVES

Brett C. Hoover

Paulist Press
New York / Mahwah, NJ

Cover image by melitas/Shutterstock.com
Cover and book design by Lynn Else

Library of Congress Cataloging-in-Publication Data
Names: Hoover, Brett C., 1967– author
Title: Immigration and faith : cultural, biblical, and theological narratives / Brett C Hoover.
Description: New York / Mahwah, NJ : Paulist Press, [2021] | Includes bibliographical references and index. | Summary: "Immigration and Faith comprehensively tackles the issues surrounding migration to and within the United States and beyond. While a suitable textbook for theology and religious studies, it goes beyond mere academic interest, calling readers to inject greater understanding into their considerations of immigration and their participation in a better future for our world"— Provided by publisher.
Identifiers: LCCN 2020037710 (print) | LCCN 2020037711 (ebook) | ISBN 9780809154739 (paperback) | ISBN 9781587688690 (ebook)
Subjects: LCSH: Emigration and immigration—Religious aspects—Christianity. | United States—Emigration and immigration.
Classification: LCC BR115.E45 H66 2021 (print) | LCC BR115.E45 (ebook) | DDC 261.8/380973—dc23
LC record available at https://lccn.loc.gov/2020037710
LC ebook record available at https://lccn.loc.gov/2020037711

ISBN 978-0-8091-5473-9 (paperback)
ISBN 978-1-58768-869-0 (e-book)

Published by Paulist Press
997 Macarthur Boulevard
Mahwah, New Jersey 07430
www.paulistpress.com

Printed and bound in the
United States of America

CONTENTS

v

CONTENTS

ACKNOWLEDGMENTS

While frequently only one name appears on the cover of a work of scholarship, it is almost never the result of only one person's wisdom and work. In the case of this work of scholarship, many people provided patient support, insights, and even necessary confrontations to make this book possible.

I have professional expressions of gratitude to offer, but I feel I must start by acknowledging my debt to friends and fellow pilgrims who taught me firsthand about migration over the years. Growing up in Southern California, I cannot remember a time when I knew no immigrants, but I am especially grateful for the friendship of both Father Gilbert Martinez, CSP, and Sister Caridad Inda, CHM, who had to endure my young ignorance but who both taught me so much. I thank migrant parishioners during my years in ministry—most immigrants but others "internal" migrants—especially those with whom I worked at St. Paul the Apostle and Holy Name of Jesus parishes in New York City. They instructed me about both the gifts and the absurdities of migration. The Mexican community at All Saints parish in the Midwest helped me during a year of research. Among many friends who are either immigrants themselves or the children of immigrants, I must acknowledge the candor of Dr. Rachel Bundang, the transparency of Olga Lucia Jaime, and constant conversation with my compadres, Dr. Cecilia Gonzalez-Andrieu and Jean Paul Andrieu. Several Black Catholic colleagues and community members over the years taught me about the importance of the Great Migration.

Many of the initial ideas behind this book emerged in conversations both long ago and relatively recently, including with several scholars and friends who did not even know I was writing this book, including Jesuit Eduardo Fernandez, Father Faustino Cruz, SM, Dr. Karen Enriquez,

Father Simon Kim, Dr. Robert Hurteau, and Father Ricky Manalo, CSP. There was an early session at the Catholic Theological Society of America where I first presented reflections on Tobit as an immigration story. In the final version of this book, I benefited not only from the persistent work of editor Diane Vescovi, but from Dr. Kristin Heyer, who reviewed my ethical reflections, from the interreligious eye of my colleague Dr. Amir Hussain, and from the more complete review of the manuscript by my colleague Dr. Nancy Pineda-Madrid, who has been writing about migration and the border for years. My wife, Shannon Green, suffered me talking about the project for a long time, and many of her thoughts and questions influenced what came to be here. Both she and Dr. Cecilia Gonzalez-Andrieu took a more serious look at the conclusion and helped me think that through.

Finally, I want to thank both graduate and undergraduate students at Loyola Marymount University in Los Angeles who took courses I taught about migration between 2016 and 2020. You will recognize the conversations we had here in these pages, and future students will benefit greatly from the questions you asked, the experiences we shared, and the thoughts you shared. I am in your debt.

Section One

MIGRATION IN RECOLLECTION AND REALITY

Remembrance of things past is not necessarily the remembrance of things as they were.

—attributed to Marcel Proust

Chapter One

MIGRATION IN RECOLLECTION

Migration produces striking and compelling human stories.

Some years back, I traveled with a small class of theology graduate students to visit a shelter for migrants in Tijuana just across the U.S.–Mexico border from San Diego. At that time, more than eighty refugees from Haiti and a handful of other nations were staying at this shelter for single men and families, awaiting word that they could line up at the San Ysidro border crossing to request asylum in the United States. When we arrived, we found dozens more than the shelter could accommodate, men and women standing outside, hoping to receive a meal and then preparing to spend the night in the street. Amid the dozens of young Haitians at the shelter, we encountered deportees as well, a small group of men forcibly separated from their families and friends in the United States. We also met a few families with teenage children fleeing the violence of organized crime in certain Pacific towns in Mexico.

After the meal, we scattered throughout the building. Almost as soon as it became clear who spoke whose language, people began to talk to us, telling us their stories, even though we were strangers. Though I do not speak Haitian Creole or French, I found myself able to communicate with many of the young Haitian refugees in Spanish. Many of them had spent months or even years crossing Latin America. They came by bus, by train, by boat, on foot. Along the way many had picked up a great deal of Spanish. Some had worked for a time in Brazil or Venezuela. Several young men related a pattern by which they would enter a country, receive a transit visa to pass through, and then move on to the next country. I also had the opportunity to listen to the stories of some of the deported men. Some had lived in the United States for more than a decade; they spoke of their lives in the north, as well as the wives and children they had left behind. One or two were surprisingly frank about the small criminal acts that got them deported. Others projected their stories into the future as they plotted their next move—to go home, to stay in Tijuana and work, to try to return to the United States. Finally, several of my students spent significant time with the Mexican families fleeing violence together. That conversation focused more on quotidian matters, though the families also speculated with my students about what their lives might become should they be granted asylum in the United States. We heard all of these stories in one twenty-four-hour visit.

NARRATIVE AND HUMAN EXPERIENCE

The experience of migration lends itself to storytelling and narrative. Migration offers up a clear plot in the world. As a geographical journey that occurs in a finite period of time, it often involves obstacles and hardships, like the heroic sagas of old. Dramatic changes in the external environments of migrants often provoke interior crisis, deeper reflection, and even transformation.[1] But migration also presents a psychological conundrum in terms of the inner life of its characters. Why would any person leave home, family, and familiar surroundings to settle in a distant place where everything is different? The act is extraordinary, risky, baffling; it strains credulity. In short, migration nearly always makes for a fascinating and compelling story, and it is no wonder that our interlocutors in Tijuana captured our attention and provoked empathy and compassion.

On a deeper level, however, neither people's desire to tell their stories nor our interest in hearing those stories should surprise us. The philosopher Paul Ricœur argues that narrative serves as a "privileged mediation" for personal and community identity.[2] "We live our lives from day to day, but we understand our life as if it were a story," says the Dutch practical theologian R. Ruard Ganzevoort.[3] The American Methodist theologian Stephen Crites goes still further, arguing that even before we make stories out of our experience, time itself imposes a kind of narrative

4

structure on our lives. One thing occurs and then another, from birth to death. When we assemble those events into a coherent story, in a sense we are only condensing the linear progression of a life. Crites concludes, "In principle, we can distinguish between the inner drama of experience and the stories through which it achieves coherence. But in any actual case the two so interpenetrate that they form a virtual identity."[4] This blurring of experience and storytelling makes intuitive sense to most of us. When I recall my younger brother's birth, I picture my sister and I watching *The Wizard of Oz* with my grandmother, but in truth I cannot meaningfully distinguish between a "real" memory and my recall of family stories about the event.

Ricœur suggests that it is precisely in the way storytelling about our experiences overtakes the experiences themselves that we discover how stories lend moral significance to our lives. The meaning of my brother's birth lies not in the exact sequence of events on that day but in the way we have turned it into a story. Ricœur refers to the work of the German literary historian Günter Müller, who contrasts narrative or "telling time" (*Erzählzeit*) with "told time" (*erzählte Zeit*), or what we might call "real time." *Erzählzeit*, or narrative time, for example, describes the seven or eight minutes it took for one of the Haitian migrants in Tijuana to tell me his story about crossing Latin America; *erzählte Zeit* is the three or four years that it actually took him to do that. Storytelling usually requires a massive condensing of time; that condensing creates what we term the *plot* of a story.[5] For Ricœur, plot becomes the instrument of a *telos*, or purpose. "Moral or ethical significance will normally come to override bare succession—that is, events occurring in mere temporal sequence—in the narrated world."[6] My Haitian interlocutor wanted me to understand what had happened to him, but he also hoped that his storytelling would evoke in me *a feel* for the existential import and moral significance of his difficult journey. His story, in that sense, had a *telos*, or purpose, far more important to him than simply communicating the details of what happened to him.

A LANDSCAPE OF NARRATIVES

The personal stories we heard in Tijuana had a powerful impact on our delegation. Because of them, we returned home with greater understanding of what migrants, refugees, and deportees suffer—crossing whole countries, helped or cheated by smugglers, escaping organized crime, forcibly separated from spouses and children. Part of the power of these stories came from the way they nuanced or even displaced other stories about immigration my students and I had heard before. None of us came to the border as blank slates regarding this issue; we had already heard plenty of stories about immigration from friends or family members, from immigrants or anti-immigrant nativists, from political leaders, in the media. We all live across a landscape of such stories, many personal and particular, but the most influential stories we call *cultural narratives*. "Narrative as an interpretive activity is mediated by cultural models of narrative sense-making that are often described as 'cultural narratives,' 'scripts,' or 'schemas.'"[7] These scripts or cultural narratives help us make sense of the events that unfold before us, but they also help us to prepare to act in response. Crites writes, "We imbibe a sense of the meaning of our own baffling dramas from these stories, and this sense of its meaning in turn affects the form of a [person's] experience and the style of his action."[8]

As we came to Tijuana hoping to understand migration better and to respond accordingly, well-known cultural narratives—even schemas or scripts we had come to doubt or discount—remained uppermost on our minds. "Cultural narratives as interpretive models affect how we experience things in the first place."[9] We listened for people speaking of coming to the United States "to seek a better life," since that "better life" story line is perhaps the most well known of cultural narratives among the *descendants* of immigrants. Perhaps some of us, with a kind of "immigrant freeloader" narrative in mind, wondered if we would hear about people crossing the border intending to take advantage of the social welfare system. Surely those we met were also monitoring these conversations with their own cultural narratives in mind—thinking that newcomers would be treated with racist contempt or perhaps that great opportunities awaited intrepid immigrants who could then return home in triumph.

Yet even as we all started with such narratives in mind, the encounter between us eventually demonstrated the inadequacies of these cultural narratives, how they sometimes relied on generalities too thin to account for the complexities of real life. In the cultural narratives we had in mind, immigrants were either good or bad, legal or illegal; people in receiving communities were either lovers or haters. It is all too simple, especially given the beguiling and heartbreaking complexities my students encountered. As a theology professor, of course, I hoped that my students would see the inadequacies of various cultural narratives and instead turn to *theological narratives* about immigration we had discussed in class, since I believed they offered greater depth and complexity, but none of us was so naïve as to think we could simply dispense with the cultural narratives. Indeed, some of my students went home only to end up arguing with family members about those same cultural narratives.

In this book, we will examine and evaluate many of the narratives that shape the way different people construct or understand migration: cultural narratives of migrants, receiving communities, and even sending communities; the "empirical narratives" put forward by the social sciences to explain the reality of migration as it emerges in data; and theological narratives from the Bible, Catholic social teaching, and other theological traditions, as well as a few from other religious traditions. My hope is that by exploring all these approaches we can not only adequately judge how accurate cultural narratives about migration are, but also deepen the resources we all have to understand the phenomenon of migration from multiple perspectives, making us better prepared to deal with migration politically, socially, ethically, and spiritually in our own societies. The kind of world we hope for is at stake. Do we want a more defensive, insular world? Would we prefer a more compassionate world with a place for everyone? How we understand and address immigration signals our trajectory as a society for the future.

MIGRATION AS KEY PLOT IN THE HUMAN STORY

I have mostly used the term *migration* here rather than *immigration*. Throughout human history people have migrated, that is, have picked up their lives and moved to other lands far away. But such movement of peoples has not always involved crossing a clear border, especially for the majority of human history during which borders shifted often or were murky or even nonexistent. Even more recently it has been possible to migrate without being an immigrant. Across the first half of the twentieth century, African American people from the rural South of the United States upended their lives, leaving behind segregation and oppression to seek a better life for themselves and their families in the more industrialized northern and western cities. Millions of people moved in this Great Migration and found themselves living in a very different cultural context. But not one of them crossed an international border. When people do cross borders as they migrate, as the patriarch Abraham does in the Book of Genesis, we call them émigrés, or immigrants, depending on which side of the border we watch from. For the people of his original homeland, Ur in Mesopotamia, Abraham simply left, became an émigré, engaged in emigration. Yet for the people who received him in the places he traveled—Haran in present-day Turkey, Egypt, and Canaan—Abraham was an immigrant. He fared better in some places than in others, and like many immigrants today, he moved on when he did not prosper.

Whether we speak of Abraham's journey from Ur to the Promised Land, or Puritans sailing to New England fleeing religious persecution, or Central American children crossing Mexico to come to live with relatives in the United States, or African Americans departing from the Jim Crow South for jobs in the North, we are telling a particular migration story, and these stories powerfully draw our attention. Because so much of human history has its roots in the movement of peoples, a lot of migration stories are *origin stories*, that is, stories that tell us how things and people came to be the way they are. Today we think of superheroes when we speak of origin stories, but they have long been with us. Biblical scholars call such stories *etiologies*, a word that comes from the Greek words for cause (*aitia*) and logic or speech (*logos*). Abraham's journey is in part an explanation of how the Israelites found themselves in the Land of Canaan, what we now call Israel, Palestine, or the Holy Land. Many of us have family origin stories that involve migration, as when my parents explained to my brother and sister and me how they migrated from the Midwest to Southern California after my mother's father died quickly and unexpectedly of pancreatic cancer. Nations tell origin stories that feature migration prominently, as when Mexicans speak of the *Mexica* people—whom we often call the Aztecs—migrating south from their original homeland until an eagle with a snake in its mouth landed on a cactus and showed them where to build their capital, Tenochtitlan, or, as it is now called, Mexico City.

The origin story of the whole human race is in part a migration story. After the first human beings evolved 2.5 million years ago, some of these first ancestors left East Africa and migrated to the Middle East, Europe, and Asia. In the mutual isolation of the various places they settled, they developed into different human species—including at least the Neanderthals (*Homo neanderthalensis*), *Homo erectus*, *Homo soloensis*, the short-of-stature *Homo floresiensis*, and *Homo denisova*. Back in East Africa, those who had stayed behind also developed into distinct species, including at least *Homo habilis*, *Home rudolfensis*, and our own species, *Homo sapiens*. A mere one hundred thousand years ago, bands of *Homo sapiens* left East Africa for the Middle East, though they apparently turned back from a land then dominated by the Neanderthals. By seventy thousand years ago, our species had experienced a "cognitive revolution" in our brains that afforded us great advantages in terms of intelligence and social skills. Some of our species then left Africa for good, and in the intervening millennia, they spread to nearly every land mass on earth, the Americas being a relative last stop less than twenty thousand years ago. Many scholars also believe that their flourishing led to the demise of other human species, either by war or by disproportionate use of resources, though traces of Neanderthal and *Homo denisova* DNA remain in people with European, Middle Eastern, Melanesian, and Aboriginal Australian ancestry. Our earliest ancestors were not too proud to breed with these other species.[10]

This grand story of human origins—what we might call the "ur-narrative" of migration—contains most of the basic elements of any migration narrative we might use today. It involves, first of all, people who left, often for complicated and sometimes inscrutable reasons. No one knows exactly why human beings left Africa. Their motivation may have come from climate change, environmental disaster, increased competition for food, or any number of reasons. Not all humans left; the story of migration is also one of people who stayed. Those of us of Amerindian, Asian, European, or Pacific Islander descent may find it easy to imagine humankind boldly setting forth from East Africa seventy thousand years ago, but Africans rightly remind us that their continent remained the original homeland of humanity, and it did not sit empty of human beings for the seventy millennia after our ancestors departed. Indeed, while an initial wave of migrants think a great deal about those they left behind, their descendants may have only the vaguest idea about them. In immigrant communities in the United States, I have witnessed tears, worry, nostalgia, and longing toward the families they left behind. I have also visited immigrants' families in Mexico, and I found them proud, happy, worried, afraid, or even resentful when thinking of those who have come north. As the generations proceed in the new country, however, people forget, almost making it feel as if the villages and towns they left no longer exist or exist in an alternative universe. The ancestors of my maternal grandfather left England for the United States in the late eighteenth century, and I can imagine their passage across the stormy Atlantic, but the village of people they left behind remains murky to me, more so the descendants who must still live there. Over time, migration creates a certain forgetfulness that those who stayed also have their stories to tell.

The human ur-narrative also draws attention to another group of people, those encountered at the destination. The Israeli historian Yuval Noah Harari notes that modern humans often envision their species developing alone in the world, but in truth *Homo sapiens* shared the world with other human species for tens of millennia. When they ventured forth from Africa, our ancestors encountered not only a myriad of other creatures, but also met other kinds of humans, interbreeding with some, competing for resources with others, perhaps killing still others in war.[11] This encounter with the human stranger already in residence remains part of migration stories today as well. As in the ancient past, newcomers and previous residents sometimes mate and marry, though at other times they suspect one another, compete for resources, or even fight. Even though most were the descendants of immigrants themselves, some Americans throughout U.S. history have treated new immigrants with contempt or suspicion, an attitude we call *nativism*, whether that nativism rejects Irish famine refugees in the 1840s or Central American children during the Trump administration. The residents that migrants encounter often hold considerable power over their fate, including their ability to achieve legal status and find employment, housing, or welcome. Refugees from the Syrian civil war of the 2010s, for example, have found that their very lives depended on the way Jordanians, Turks, and Europeans received them.

Thus, in a short retelling of human origins, we already see all of the key "characters" for which a good migration narrative accounts—not only the migrants, but those left behind and those encountered at the destination. At the same time, the context of ancient human origins allows us to contemplate the experience of these characters at a safe distance, historical and emotional. Few of us will have strong reactions to millennia-old migration stories, unless we are Christian fundamentalists denying the reality of human evolution or paleoanthropologists arguing over the proper interpretation of it. Yet even at a safe distance we recognize that these migration stories tell us something about human identity. Both movement and stability have defined us; we are *homo manetor* and *homo migrator*. Such an observation, of course, is so general and the story that engenders it so remote that almost no one is likely to dispute it.

As the historical and emotional distance between us and the migration stories that we tell recedes, however, the stories do not feel safe at all. Listening to the stories of Syrian refugees in Jordanian refugee camps, U.S. white nationalists' pejorative accounts of Mexican immigration, or the complicated reports of Filipino children regarding their parents' work abroad, it becomes difficult to remain impassive or to accept the meaning of the stories as straightforward. The human immediacy draws our attention, but such stories also touch our sense of identity more directly. Arriving Syrian refugees alter the demographic realities of towns and cities and sometimes frighten those who have little experience with Muslims. White nationalists blanket the internet with a vision of the United States as principally for whites. Filipino children missing their immigrant parents arouse our complex feelings about childhood and parenthood.[12] Faced with these kinds of stories, few people can maintain a cool neutrality. Indeed, in a world where millions migrate every year, everyone's life feels touched by migration in some way. We are implicated; we not only care but also feel angst about how these stories speak of who we are.

In such moments, theologian Michele Saracino warns that human beings have a tendency to invest too much in a single narrative, to treat a cultural narrative as the "one true story" of a phenomenon to the exclusion of all others. In her book *Being about Borders*, Saracino identifies this as a primary concern, for example, in the relationship between mothers and their children; for many people there is only one way to understand motherhood, and those who eschew it, for example, by admitting to ambivalence over childbearing and rearing, deserve stern judgment. Saracino finds the "one true story" problem at work in the tensions between Jews and Christians over who Jesus is, and between Jewish Israelis and Arab Palestinians over the meaning of the land. Across these contexts, she worries about the way in which an idealized story represents an idealized self, a narcissistic projection designed to protect our fragile self-esteem against the intrusive demands of the others in our lives, people both similar to us and different at the same time.[13] Indeed, the emotional vulnerability and identity confusion introduced by migration makes it prime territory for constructing the "one true story." Such a narrative then makes it difficult for even fellow religionists to have a clear, tradition-rooted conversation about it.[14] Many of the cultural and theological narratives in this book became "one true stories" at one point or another, and much of the conversation to come explores how and why they became so exclusive that they put an end to conversation. One of the simpler explanations has to do with the way we *remember* migration.

MIGRATION AND MEMORY

Migration stories, ancient or modern, demonstrate something about the dynamic of memory. When we tell any story about what has happened to us personally or collectively, we are, as Ricœur noted, condensing the past, in a sense, stringing our memories of the past together in a coherent way. But remembering the past remains tricky. Decades ago, the pioneering work of the psychologist Elizabeth Loftus exposed the reconstructive nature of eyewitness testimony. She found that we do not draw from our brains some kind of film reel of what happened; rather, we reconstruct as we remember, shaping the story, filling in the gaps. Various factors shape that process of reconstruction, such as mood, expectations, intervening events, and cultural narratives and schemas, though actual events have a certain staying power in the midst of these factors.[15] All this is to say that many things influence the way people reconstruct migration stories, whether such narratives be personal, familial, or cultural.

Growing up I heard my parents recount our family's big move from Indiana to California in the 1960s. Each time it could sound a little different. Sometimes it followed the larger cultural narrative of the Sun Belt migration at the time, of people fleeing colder climates for the warm zones of the South and Southwest. My father would speak of disembarking from an airplane for a job interview and feeling overwhelmed by the bright sunlight; both he and my mother declared they would never shovel snow again. Other times the story had overtones of my parents having "escaped" from the town in which they grew up. Especially in the 1970s, while racial tensions remained consistently in the news, my mom would describe the racist language she heard growing up. She hoped we would grow up in a different kind of world. If either of my parents were thinking of my mother's father, a beloved figure to both, the story would emphasize his death from pancreatic cancer and my grandmother's grief-filled flight to Los Angeles, preceding them. In some sense, all of these accounts tell a piece of the truth, but they all emphasize different aspects of our family's journey and nuance the motivation for that journey in different ways. None of them is a detailed chronology of what happened; all remain reconstructions.

The longer the interval between an experience and retelling the experience, the more numerous the lacunae, or gaps, that require more imaginative reconstruction. When I supervise students engaging in participant observation of faith communities, I encourage them to compile their narratives of the experience (field notes) as soon as humanly possible after their visit; otherwise, they forget the details. Not surprisingly, the further back a family's migration experience lies, the more lacunae there are in the retelling of it. If an experience of immigration was traumatic or painful, parents may consciously decide to omit many details when recounting it to their children. My grandfather once told me how his German neighbors suddenly ceased to speak German as the United States entered the Second World War in 1941, and indeed many families lost track of their German language and culture during the two world wars. They never spoke of how they came to the United States. Even without such dramatic events, over the generations, the circumstances of migration can seem murkier and murkier.

Over the generations, memory gaps around migration can grow so enormous that we might speak of *immigrant amnesia*, a gradual and near complete erasing of a family or community's memory regarding the migration experience. This experience appears pervasive among European Americans whose ancestors arrived in the United States more than a generation or two ago.[16] My ancestors came to this country from England, Ireland, and Germany, somewhere between five and ten generations ago. Genetic tests confirm this, but we have little to no information about any of these ancestors or about why they embarked on such a fraught journey. A distant relative claims that ancestors of my paternal grandmother came to the United States in 1870 so that their young sons would not be drafted into the German (formerly the Prussian) army. But I have little sense of whether this is true, or if that family really lies in a direct line back from mine.

To admit such uncertainty, however, is not easy or fashionable. Because most human beings think of their ancestry as having implications for their identity, uncertainty about our past can feel costly, and many of us who suffer from immigrant amnesia hold on to the scraps of reports from the past as gospel, even if we have little explicit evidence that they are true. Most of us go beyond even this, reconstructing our ancestors' immigrant pasts using cultural narratives we adapt to the occasion. We might call this *immigrant nostalgia*, and it usually paints our own ancestors in a flattering—if perhaps romanticized—light, sometimes with a subtext criticizing immigrants today. I have had many conversations with fellow European Americans who insist vociferously that their ancestors left their homelands to definitively "become American," that they came in an orderly and *legal* way, and that they learned English with astonishing speed. In truth, such claims are more a product of today's controverted climate around immigration than they are an expression of the historical record. Historical accounts, in fact, often contradict these claims. Nineteenth-century and early twentieth-century immigrants came for as many complicated reasons as people today. Almost half of Southern and Eastern European immigrants of the early twentieth century, excepting Ashkenazi Jews fleeing persecution, came to work and then returned home.[17] Before 1924, there existed no category of entering legally or illegally, so ancestors who came before then could not claim that alleged moral high ground. Finally, in reality, more immigrants speak English today than did around 1900.[18]

The larger cultural narratives that build up our immigrant nostalgia, filling in the gaps for our immigrant amnesia, are paradoxically themselves shaped by amnesia or nostalgia. When those of us of European American extraction argue that our ancestors came pursuing an American Dream of social mobility, we are often nostalgically projecting the postwar rise of the middle class back into the nineteenth or early twentieth century. Amnesia about the lower social mobility of that earlier time permits that projection. Racism produces a different sort of amnesia across U.S. history, one that erases the reality of African ancestry in the lives of many people who identify as white, replacing a complicated story—whose plot points could include master-slave rape, interracial adultery, or racial "passing"—with less complicated versions that nostalgically emphasize European migration stories.[19] The tumult of the Mexican Revolution (1910–17) provoked a great deal of migration to the United States, though the details were often lost to history in many families. Nostalgia about the role of that revolution in Mexican identity has helped construct a widespread cultural narrative regarding Mexican Americans' ancestors' participation in the revolution. To posit otherwise would be to edit one's family out of a crucial event for national and ethnic identity, but not everyone's great-grandfather could have ridden with Pancho Villa.

Even when generations have not passed, amnesia or nostalgia may seep into cultural migration narratives. The theologian Simon Kim describes how Korean immigrants of a certain generation do not speak to their children of the poverty or political repression that prompted their departure from South Korea decades ago. Instead, they hope their children's success will release them from their own "broken-heartedness" (Korean *han*). Their children, witnessing the "Asian tiger" economy of South Korea today, listening to K-pop, and watching K-drama on television, may have a rather romanticized notion about the Korea their families left behind.[20] Amnesia and nostalgia may even infect the memories not of migrants but of those who remained in the homeland. A decade ago, I traveled to Mexico and visited the families and neighbors of immigrants I knew from a Catholic parish in the Midwest. In one town, the economy was prospering, and family members had lost track of the economic difficulties that had prompted their relatives and friends to depart in the first place. Those who decided to return often spoke of the discrimination they suffered in the United States, and that narrative of rejection often overshadowed the stability and relative happiness their U.S. family members actually experienced.

MIGRATION NARRATIVES

By examining the way migration narratives work, and by exposing the strategies of amnesia and nostalgia they depend on, my intention is not simply to demonstrate the inadequacy of these narratives. If narrative is, as Ricœur says, condensed reality, all accounts of migration will fail to capture some aspect of migration's complex dynamics. The ethicist

Tisha Rajendra notes, "Any narrative necessarily includes some details and omits others; some facts, perspectives, and insights are emphasized while others may be de-emphasized or omitted entirely....Narratives must strive for fidelity to reality, though they will ultimately fall short."[21] No story will be complete. Nor do I intend to simply expose the historical inconsistencies in many migration stories as a way of criticizing our faulty memories. If all memory has a reconstructive element, and many of these stories depend on events long past, some forms of amnesia and nostalgia are inevitable. The literary critic Svetlana Boym, however, argues that not all forms of nostalgia serve the individual or the common good.[22] While part of the work within these pages is to understand migration and the narratives that shape our perception of it, the more important task is to determine whether and how these narratives and the perceptions they engender serve the common good. That common good includes all three of the communities involved in each migration narrative—the migrant community, the receiving community, and the community that remains behind in the country of origin. Since this book is a work of Christian theology, we will examine this question primarily through a Christian lens, with reference to the other religions, especially Judaism and Islam, but also Buddhism and Hinduism, as well.

Such an approach places this work squarely within the tradition of practical theology. In practical theology, sometimes described as pastoral theology in Catholic circles, we begin with a description and analysis of the concrete challenges that confront us as Christians. The liberation theologian Ignacio Ellacuría calls this "grasping what is at stake in reality" (in Spanish, *hacerse cargo de la realidad*).[23] In this case, we attempt to unpack the complex challenge that is contemporary migration to North America, particularly the United States. The next chapter of this work summarizes the history of immigration to the United States and gathers sociological data on migration today, including a presentation of important theoretical perspectives that help us make sense of that data. The history and the sociology will help us understand the different kinds of migrants, some of the reasons people migrate, as well as those factors that favor or inhibit their integration into U.S. society. That chapter includes a look at the development of immigration law in the United States.

The two chapters in the second section explore the cultural narratives that have shaped public understanding of migration: the first chapter of these explores the cultural narratives of receiving communities, such as the "better life," or American Dream narrative; the second chapter looks at the stories of migrants and sending communities, including more temporary and provisional versions of the "better life" narrative, as well as narratives of escape or flight, and rejection narratives that contend with the suspicion and opposition some migrants experience. The second of these chapters will also, to a lesser extent, take note of the cultural narratives of communities that remain in the home country. These communities' narratives are shaped by both the promise of migration and the sense of void or loss left by those who go.

Chapters 5 and 6 comprise the third section, and they explore the narratives and schemas about migration found, or at least implied, in sacred texts of some of the world's most influential religious traditions. Chapter 5 takes a broader, interreligious look, examining how religious traditions treat the journey of life itself and how that impacts their narratives about migration. Chapter 6 focuses on the Hebrew Bible, known by Christians as the Old Testament, and the Christian New Testament. Most of the narratives in this chapter center on welcoming the migrant and the migrant's role as God's messenger, but a lesser strain of stories also exists that demonstrates more caution or even hostility toward the stranger. All of this scriptural background helps us begin to make sense of the previously considered cultural narratives and the attitudes and behaviors they evoke. The fourth and final section begins with a chapter exploring the way biblical reflections on migration were taken up by the early theologians of Christianity, following that trajectory through medieval theology, especially in the West, and narratives of migration formed in the wake of the global intercultural encounters of the sixteenth century and beyond. That chapter ends with a consideration of the Catholic social teaching on migration that formed across the twentieth century. This will open up an account of contemporary approaches to migration in Christian ethics, many of which are strongly influenced by Catholic social teaching or by biblical teaching. Finally, we look at theological approaches to migration from outside of ethics, concluding with a "practical theology of migration" that pulls together the previous reflections. The intent is not to formulate some sort of migration super-narrative, an amalgamation of all that has come before, but to summarize what we can learn from all these narratives, judged in the light of the reign of God, the eschatological trajectory of the Christian gospel. This will lead to some modest proposals for the reform of Christian practice around migration, intended not only for believing Christians and Christian faith communities, but also for persons of no religion, who nevertheless search for a humane and just way to understand migration and find love in their hearts for the stranger in their midst.

TOBIT'S RECAPITULATION

I conclude this first chapter as I began it, with a collection of migration stories, in this case from a little-known fable from the intertestamental period, that is, the time between the writing of the Hebrew Bible and the New Testament. A diaspora story originally written in Aramaic, the lingua franca of the ancient Near East, the Book of Tobit found its way into the Greek translation of the Hebrew Bible, the Septuagint, and subsequently into the Catholic and Orthodox Bibles. It remains part of the Apocrypha in the Bibles of the Reformation traditions. Tobit chronicles the lives of Tobit; his wife, Anna; their son, Tobiah; and Tobiah's wife, Sarah, all refugees of the Assyrian conquest of the Northern Kingdom of Israel. Its loose sense of the history of that time reveals how its actual origins lie many centuries later, making it a work born in immigrant amnesia and fortified by immigrant nostalgia. Perhaps as a result, the Book of Tobit reads as a fanciful story, even outrageously so. Bird droppings prompt blindness; archangels guide travelers; foul-smelling incense expels a curiously dangerous demon. Even in the midst of the fantastical elements, and at a considerable historical remove from the actual events, the story still offers a vivid feel for the actual experience and consequences of migration and exile. I think of it as the paradigmatic myth of migration, inasmuch as we understand *myth* as an ancient story intended to evoke both empathy and understanding of one of the basic phenomena of human life. The Book of Tobit portrays the practical dilemmas of migrants, divisions within their diasporic communities, the cruelties inflicted by fearful receiving communities, and the transnational landscape that migration produces. In short, it condenses and recapitulates many of the factors necessary for understanding a good migration narrative.

Like all refugees and some migrants today, Tobit and Anna do not leave their homeland voluntarily. Born in the Northern Kingdom of Israel, they experience the destruction of that kingdom in 722 BCE by the Assyrians and are forcibly exiled along with many of their relatives and fellow Israelites. Like many refugees and exiles, Tobit deposits money in varied places to ensure he does not lose everything amid the catastrophe of flight. They end up in Nineveh, the imperial capital and economic center of the Assyrians and where their economic fortunes wax and wane. Like most migrants, they remain ever vulnerable to political and economic fluctuations. In good times and in bad, like many immigrants I have met, Tobit gives generously to the needy, especially those among his own people.

Tobit firmly decides that he and Anna should keep faithful to their culture and religion, that they should not totally assimilate (Anna seems not so sure), though he works for the government for a short while until he loses his prestigious job. Others of their tribe opt to assimilate, hoping to keep their heads down and avoid trouble, a choice symbolized by their abandonment of the Jewish dietary laws. Tobit, on the other hand, holds firmly to his Israelite identity, even when he finds that his commitment to ancestral customs and traditions brings him into risky conflict with the government. Night after night, he secretly buries and prays over dead compatriots, their bodies left in the street, murdered by the regime. His good deeds result in mistrust and persecution on the part of his new neighbors, who do not understand what he does.

Ultimately, Tobit seems sure even God has abandoned him, when he is struck blind (by the aforementioned bird poop), just as many migrants and refugees today find themselves confronted by unexpected illnesses and injuries they are ill-prepared to confront. As Tobit and Anna's troubles mount, marital discord ensues, just as in many immigrant households under pressure. Eventually Tobit and Anna abandon all hope for their own success and focus their attention on their only child, Tobiah. They urge him not to be tempted to the vices that abound in their new home and to remain faithful to their family, culture, and heritage. Tobit's speech to his son sounds remarkably like an instruction one might hear from the parents of any child growing up in a new nation with its own risks and temptations.

Tobiah then becomes a "voluntary" migrant, undertaking a dangerous journey into yet another country, Media. He goes on a quest for material resources in search of a "better life" for his family, with the intention of returning soon. Like many migrants today, he does so believing that God goes with him, represented in this case by the arch-angel Raphael, disguised as the merchant and guide Azariah. While in Media he meets a woman from his own people and falls in love with her, an eventuality in almost any immigrant community. Before they can marry, together they must withstand the demonic powers who have thwarted Sarah's previous attempts at marital happiness; the demon Asmodeus has killed seven previous suitors. Perhaps here we can find a parallel to the seemingly demonic discrimination today's migrants suffer, or a sign of the way marital bliss can be thwarted by the complications of migration, from the deportation of one partner to economic struggles to confusion and envy brought on by changing gender roles in the new country.

In Tobiah and Sarah's case, they pray to persevere. Aided by Raphael's home remedy of burnt fish liver, they send the demon into flight to Egypt. In this story, even the demons are migrants! Like an Interpol police officer seeking the extradition of a criminal, the angel Raphael goes after him and eventually "arrests" him (binds him up) in the desert. Tobiah and Sarah finish celebrating their marriage, and they return to Nineveh to take care of Tobit and Anna and to raise a large family in their multigenerational household, echoing the house-hold arrangements of many immigrants today. Raphael finally reveals himself as God's messenger. For years afterward, the extended family lives together in relative quiet until Tobit and Anna die, still in exile in Nineveh. Soon Tobiah and Sarah find that they must relocate their family again, as political turmoil shakes the Assyrian Empire. No one in the family ever returns to the land of Israel.

The story of Tobit's family—even with the absurdist elements of blindness induced by bird droppings, husband-killing demons, demon-destroying fish liver incense, and archangels in disguise—often parallels quotidian elements in the stories of today's migrants and refugees. They also suffer forced relocation, migrate looking for financial help intending to return, react to political turmoil and eco-nomic changes, and struggle to withstand temptations and hold on to their culture and faith in a foreign land. Like Tobit, Anna, Tobiah, and Sarah, they respond to these challenges with pragmatism and faith. More like Tobit and less like the archetypal and wealthy Abraham, today's migrants suffer unpredictable reversals of fortune. Some people they encounter at their destination suspect them, while others wel-come them. They detect divine accompaniment along their journey, hidden at first and then revealed in hindsight, just as Tobiah's traveling companion Azariah finally reveals himself as the archangel Raphael, "one of the seven angels who stand ready and enter before the glory of the Lord" (Tobit 12:15).

The name Raphael in Hebrew means "God is healer," and indeed, there is much pain and grief in the experience of migrants, and often also in the experience of those receiving them and those left behind. The demon's name in the story, Asmodeus, is an Aramaic adaptation of the ancient Persian words for "demon of wrath."[24] Very often cultural narratives about migration communicate how migration can *feel* like an apocalyptic struggle, angels and demons at war around us. Indeed, many personal stories I have heard confirm this. While this tells us something important about the emotional intensity of the experience, and the danger posed by the intense fears migration appears to generate, such an apocalyptic account can also obscure the complexity of what actually happens and why. In the next chapter, the history and social science of migration supplies us with a deeper account of that complexity.

Chapter Two

MIGRATION IN REALITY

In the last chapter, we saw how migration often comes to our attention as a story. That story can be told by migrants but also by the communities that send or receive them. When it is someone's personal story, we learned, it may be poignant and change our hearts, but personal stories can also be forgotten over time or regenerated by later generations to prove a point. Migration also comes to us in cultural narratives, the big stories of "seeking a better life" or "immigrant threat" that are shared by an entire culture or community. Such narratives prove influential, but they are also subject to human error and fading memories. We also found that migration has remained part of the greater human story from the very beginnings of our species, and it has appeared in the scriptures of many religions, including Christianity. We concluded with the migration story of Tobit in the Catholic and Orthodox Bibles, finding that many of its twists and turns echo the concerns of migrants today. But other aspects of Tobit's story remain just fanciful, a wild tale from a different era. Indeed, if we want to understand migration well, we have to turn our attention not only to these stories but to its historical and contemporary reality. And so we consult the data and interpretations of historians, regarding migration in the past, and social scientists, regarding the mechanics of migration today, to help us understand migration in reality and to see how well it compares to our stories and narratives.

MIGRATION BY THE NUMBERS

Statistics show that human beings continue to migrate, perhaps in larger numbers than ever. In 2017, a total of 258 million people migrated from one country to another, about one out of every twenty-nine persons on earth. Yet, as the demographer Ronald Skeldon points out, this number almost certainly represents an undercount, since it does not take into account those persons who return to the countries from which they came. That is, it leaves out multitudes, such as the nearly half of all Italian migrants to the United States from 1890 to 1920, who for varied reasons decided to go home. International migration data also shows nothing about internal migrants, people who uproot their lives but migrate within national borders. In 2000, the United Nations estimated that at least 740 million people had moved from one region to another within their countries.[1]

As incomplete as UN data on migration might seem, this information gives us some sense of the vast scope of migration as a phenomenon. People migrate, for example, at a rate that is growing faster than the world's population. As most North Americans would probably expect, most (64 percent) of today's migrants move to high-income nations, such as the United States, Canada, Japan, South Korea, Bahrain, or in Western Europe, though not all of them come from poorer nations. The two biggest migration flows, for example, are not from Latin America to the United States or from Africa to Europe, but from one Asian country to another or from one European country to another. Almost a third of migrants find their way to what the World Bank calls middle-income countries like Mexico, India, Indonesia, or Nigeria. The U.S. State Department estimates that up to 1.5 million U.S. citizens live in Mexico.[2] Twenty source nations account for almost half of all international migrants, but that number includes not only desperately poor nations like Bangladesh or Afghanistan but also Germany and the United Kingdom.[3] Among the ten nations that receive more than half of all international migrants, all are relatively well-off, Russia and Spain being the least affluent.[4] The biggest nation-to-nation migration flows in 2017 contain fewer surprises—from Mexico to the

United States, from India to the United Arab Emirates, back and forth between Russia and Ukraine (with all the complex political implications there), from Syria to Turkey, and from Bangladesh to India.[5]

Migration is grand and complicated, but its prominence as a topic for discussion, and the strength of opinions on it, may make it seem bigger than it actually is. More than 95 percent of the world's population have never moved from one country to another. Migration undoubtedly has a larger profile in big destination countries like the United States or Canada, but even there it may seem bigger than it really is. The U.S. Census Bureau calculated that 13.2 percent of the U.S. population was born in another country, according to data collected from 2012 to 2017, slightly more than one out of every eight people. This is actually lower than the ratio at its historical heights during the immigration waves of the late nineteenth and early twentieth centuries. In a 2018 survey of people in six nations, Americans estimated the immigrant population to be three times its actual size.[6] Nevertheless, in the living memory of older Americans, the foreign-born population has increased dramatically, from less than 5 percent of the population in 1970 to the current 13.2 percent, according to the Census Bureau. Most immigrants in 1970 were of European descent; in 2010, over 80 percent were from Latin America or Asia.[7] Even in the so-called gateway cities and states, the population of immigrants half a century ago was much lower than it is now. Just under 9 percent of the population of California in 1970 was born in another country. By 2010, almost 30 percent of the population of California was foreign born.[8]

Statistics hint at the scope and complexity of migration, but they ultimately do not tell us what we might call an empirical story of migration, that is, how and why it happens and what the consequences might be for migrants, those who receive them, and those left behind in sending nations. To offer an empirical account of migration here, we focus on the U.S. experience. First, we review the history of migration in the United States, including a brief tour of immigration law, which has been far more deeply intertwined with the history of racial and ethnic discrimination than some might expect. Next, we examine some of the most influential social scientific explanations for why people migrate at the macro and local levels. Finally, we explore the phenomenon of immigrant adaptation to U.S. society, including changes in the notion of "assimilation" in social science.

Although the U.S. experience remains somewhat unique, these explanations begin to uncover the dynamics of migration in other parts of the world, as well.

NATION OF IMMIGRANTS

A few years ago, my wife's parents came to visit, and we all got into her Volkswagen to visit a local restaurant. As we drove out of our neighborhood, we passed a house with a prominent lawn sign. I had never seen the sign before, even though I walked past this house with some regularity. The sign urged an immediate end to illegal immigration and the prompt deportation of anyone here without papers. This was before the Trump campaign in 2016. Especially in multicultural Southern California where I lived, one did not often see such naked support for getting rid of ten or eleven million people at once. Such an undertaking would require a near-impossible logistical effort and probably trillions of dollars. The sign also reminded me of the frequent racial tint to such a call. People who advocate for this do not imagine unauthorized Canadians or Polish people, who do in fact exist, but rather they want to get rid of Mexicans, occasionally Central Americans. All of this must have shown on my face in that moment. My wife's stepfather, who was born on the Fort Peck Indian Reservation in eastern Montana and is an enrolled member of the Assiniboine and Sioux tribes there, quickly announced to the three white people in the car, "Well, we tried that with you all, but it didn't work."

In the previous chapter, we saw how immigrant families, suffering the anguish and stress of adapting to a new land, often fail to impress upon their descendants the difficulties and complexity of their experience. After a few generations, the descendants of immigrants suffering from a combination of amnesia and nostalgia know little about the immigrant experience of their ancestors. The long period of lower immigration to the United States, from 1920 into the 1960s, exacerbated that process of forgetting and romanticizing for the descendants of European immigrants. As a result, European Americans today often know little about what migration is like. This makes it far easier to adhere to sweeping generalizations about, for example, unauthorized immigrants today.

In the previous chapter, we saw that migration is a story not only about migrants but also about receiving and sending communities. The experience of the latter two in the past often goes unreported, in part because of the gradual amnesia that develops among migrant-descended communities as they adapt to life in their new home. A critical history of immigration then serves as an important corrective to these gaps and reconstructions in our family and community memories. It asks migrants, sending communities, and receiving communities, as well as the descendants of all three, to pause before making generalizations about the phenomenon of migration. It especially compels the grandchildren, great-grandchildren, or great-great-grandchildren of immigrants to stop and think before declaiming that "my ancestors came legally" or "they learned to speak English." Did they really learn to speak English? How quickly? Was there such a thing as coming legally or illegally in their time? Consulting historical sources allows us to see more of what *was* rather than what we believe should have been.

My father-in-law's comment reminded me of a foundational fact about migration to North America. It began not with the arrival of Europeans but with the arrival of Asiatic peoples many, many millennia ago. Our knowledge of that story is still developing, but it seems that by thirteen thousand years ago, human beings had spread across most of the Americas.[9] By the sixteenth and seventeenth centuries of our era, European migrants arrived in lands that for millennia had belonged to hundreds of distinct indigenous nations, people largely isolated from the other peoples of the world during that time. These receiving communities did not fare well. The long isolation left the people we now call Native Americans (generally known as American Indians among their own, or as First Nations in Canada, or *indígenas* in Latin American Spanish or Portuguese) with little to no immunity to the diseases of Europeans. Thus, one of the first tragic consequences of the arrival of the Europeans was the spread of lethal plagues. Death literally made space for Europeans, but eventually, as far as the European settlers were concerned, not enough. Over time settlers forced many indigenous nations to migrate themselves, many in forced relocation marches—the Cherokee Trail of Tears is only the most well known—that led to more deaths.

Indeed, we might say that the colonial history of migration in North America is largely three histories: (1) the migration of settlers from England, France, Spain, and Latin America; (2) repeated coercive relocation of receiving indigenous communities; and (3) kidnapping and "importation" of Africans to work as chattel slaves. After the thirteen colonies along the Eastern Seaboard rebelled and formed a new country, the latter two forced migrations continued, the last illegally after 1808, when constitutional prohibitions on the slave trade took effect. The Atlantic slave trade also raises the difficult and complex topic of the "sending community" in West Africa. On the one hand, some Africans participated in the slave trade, and slavery existed in some African societies, albeit in a nonracialized form. But the cruelty of the Atlantic slave trade established by Europeans was something altogether terrible and different. It was felt acutely in those parts of sub-Saharan Africa subjected to continual slave raids. Families and communities lost loved ones and neighbors, and their own histories and livelihoods were altered by that reality.[10]

The impact on sending communities proved less dramatic in Europe, where more "push" factors, such as population density, inadequate economic opportunities, recruitment of indentured servants, and the desire to exile convicts, drove migration to the Americas. Many of us of European descent might be surprised to learn that our ancestors were indentured servants or even convicts! Early on, even before the American Revolution, settlers began to arrive in English North America not only from England but from Ireland, Scotland, and Germany. In 1753, as more Germans came to Pennsylvania, Benjamin Franklin praised Germans' farming skills but complained of their "ignorance" and lack of respect for church leaders.[11] Also, before the Revolution, French-speaking Acadians deported from British Canada moved in large numbers to Louisiana, which became part of the new country in 1804.

After 1820, European immigrants began to come to the United States in great numbers, particularly Irish and German people. Irish immigration numbers rose dramatically during the Great Potato Famine of the 1840s, when emigration provided one of the few alternatives to starvation. For the most part, Irish people settled in U.S. cities, contributing to American industrialization, while Germans moved to cities and rural destinations in an area of the Midwest (then called "the West") that became known as the German triangle. In general, the two groups had radically different attitudes toward adaptation. By this time, most Irish were English speaking. They favored more rapid assimilation, perhaps in part as a response to a wave of anti-Irish and anti-Catholic politics, which reached its zenith with the rise of a nativist political party, the American Party, also known as the Know Nothings. Several convents and Catholic churches were burned. Germans, who were Catholic or Protestant, preferred to speak their own language and adapt more gradually. In one Midwestern town, a city councilman told me his ancestors spoke German for six generations in the United States, until the two world wars made the language suspect.[12] Meanwhile, additional Indian nations were forcibly relocated to less settled territories like Kansas and Oklahoma.

From the sixteenth century through the early nineteenth century, Spanish-speaking settlers from Spain and Latin America began to populate the northern frontiers of Spain's colonial empire. Many of the settlers to California were of African descent and found greater freedom from discrimination in frontier towns like Los Angeles.[13] In 1820, these northern territories became part of the new nation of Mexico. From 1846 to 1848, the United States fought a lopsided war against the young nation, taking its northern half upon victory. The 1848 Treaty of Guadalupe-Hidalgo made thousands of Mexicans into U.S. citizens, many unwillingly. In California and Texas, their lands were often expropriated by Anglo settlers through protracted court battles. The discovery of gold in California in 1849, and the construction of the transcontinental railroad during the 1860s, brought significant numbers of Chinese immigrants to the United States for the first time. Anti-Chinese violence eventually erupted, and a political movement emerged toward the exclusion of immigrants from China and eventually all of East Asia, which found political success beginning in the 1880s.[14]

Also, during the 1880s, the source nations of European immigration began to shift. Immigrants from southern and eastern Europe came, some of them with families hoping to settle, but almost 40 percent were single men seeking work. Often recruited by American companies, many returned home once they had earned enough money. Jewish immigrants came in large numbers escaping the pogroms of the Russian Empire; they did not return to Europe.[15] This new wave of migrants also encountered an anti-immigrant backlash in receiving communities, which took on racial overtones during the early decades of the twentieth century. Certain scholars asserted the inferiority of darker-skinned immigrants from Asia and southern Europe, and the reborn Ku Klux Klan, spurred to popularity in part by D.W. Griffith's film *Birth of a Nation*, whipped up sentiment against immigrant Jews and Catholics, as well as against African Americans. By the 1920s, the nativist backlash had inspired a series of restrictionist laws, and immigration largely came to a standstill for decades.

In part as a response to the ensuing labor shortages during that time, a wave of African American migrants came from the rural South to industrial and service jobs in the northern and western cities. Initially set off by northern labor shortages during the First World War, the Great Migration was also precipitated by the persistent, oppressive Southern caste system known collectively by the moniker Jim Crow. The early twentieth-century version of the caste system proved particularly brutal. Restricted from economic advancement, African Americans in the South faced underfunded segregated schools, legal restrictions against the use of public facilities enjoyed by whites, relegation in shops and restaurants to the back door, the back kitchen, the back of the line, and the back of the bus. Crimes both real and, more often, imagined—the latter usually involving Black men's alleged interest in white women—led to the extrajudicial killing (or "lynching") of thousands of African Americans, the murders often turning into a spectacle or social event. By the time the Great Migration ended in the 1970s, almost half of African Americans lived beyond the South, compared to just 10 percent near the beginning of the century. The flow of persons and information back and forth between North and South also helped spur the Civil Rights Movement.[16]

Labor shortages during the Second World War precipitated another wave of migration, this time from Mexico. With so many young men mobilized for war, the U.S. government negotiated with Mexico to recruit thousands of manual laborers, *braceros*, to fill agricultural and industrial jobs. There had already been a surge of migration from Mexico during the 1910s and 1920s, as the tumult of the Mexican Revolution and then the *Cristero* conflict turned thousands of Mexicans into refugees, though hundreds of thousands, including U.S. citizens, were also deported during the Great Depression. The *bracero* program continued after the war, and even when it ceased in 1964, U.S. agribusiness and other employers had come to rely on Mexican labor, often underpaid. Mexican laborers continued to come to the United States, but more now without papers. Many moved back and forth across the border. Periodic crackdowns continued, the most comprehensive in 1954. By the 1980s, however, the large number of unauthorized immigrants led the U.S. Congress and the Republican Reagan administration to arrange for a large-scale amnesty in exchange for changes in the laws making it harder for unauthorized immigrants to find work.

By the 1980s, the demographic profile of immigration had changed dramatically; the new immigrants came not from Europe but from Latin America, Mexico in particular, as well as from the Pacific Islands and Asia. The movement of peoples encouraged transnational exchanges—of money, products, culture—between such places and the United States, cementing relationships begun in economic or political colonialism. Beginning in the 1970s and 1980s, abetted by Cold War competition between the United States and the Soviet Union, civil wars erupted across Central America, leading to an influx of refugees and migrants from El Salvador, Nicaragua, and Guatemala. Koreans, Vietnamese, Cambodians, and Hmong people came as refugees after the Korean and Vietnam Wars. Over time, family reunification policies brought whole families. Immigrants also began to come from China in larger numbers. While Filipino laborers had come to fill agricultural labor shortages early in the twentieth century, now professionals, especially doctors and nurses, were recruited or welcomed. Professionals from India and Pakistan not only found opportunities in engineering and technology sectors but also in founding small businesses. Most Asian immigrants opted to settle on the West Coast or in New York City.

The 1980s and 1990s also brought a new wave of nativism, a contempt or suspicion of immigrants, to the United States. As demographic changes altered the ethnic and racial makeup of California, for example, a collection of wealthy conservatives initiated organized efforts designed to pressure unauthorized immigrants to leave. Proposition 187 banned unauthorized immigrants and their children from receiving many government services and required hospitals and schools to report them. Though it passed, courts quickly declared most if its provisions unconstitutional. The main consequence of this and other initiatives was to mobilize Latinx voters in California against the Republican Party, effectively delivering the state to Democratic control for decades to come. The Clinton administration, working with a Republican Congress after 1994, made it more difficult for immigrants to receive government benefits and stepped up enforcement at the southern border. The latter move had the paradoxical effect of keeping undocumented immigrants in the United States, as it became increasingly difficult and even dangerous to cross back and forth. This, in turn, drove up the price of illegally crossing the border to astronomical new heights. Nativism eventually reached its zenith during the Trump administration, when Attorney General Jeff Sessions presided over the first of many attempts to increase deportations of unauthorized immigrants and to drastically limit the number of refugees and immigrants entering legally.

A SHORT HISTORY OF IMMIGRATION LAW

Understanding this complicated history requires reckoning with the legal structures that both shaped and were shaped by the phenomenon of migration to the United States. Immigration law has a certain notoriety for its mind-boggling complexity. As I briefly noted in the previous chapter, in the 1870s, young men in the family of my grandmother's German ethnic ancestors were not permitted to leave Germany, probably because they were of age for military service, but the family apparently smuggled them out anyway, and they found no bar to entry on the U.S. side. More recently, a Filipino family I know was able to procure visas to immigrate after the father worked some years for the U.S. government in the Philippines. Many other Filipinos, often siblings or adult children of Filipino American citizens, face a wait of ten to twenty years to gain permission to come. Some asylum seekers are released with orders to report periodically while others remain in detention for months or even years. One Colombian woman I knew in New York City was able to receive a green card and eventually U.S. citizenship, while another languished in the shadows with no perceived path to regularizing her status. What are we to make of these seeming contradictions and absurdities?

Part of the reason immigration law remains so complicated—often to the point of absurdity—is because it is the result of many different laws passed across the landscape of American history. Especially compared with many other nations, the United States has had a relatively welcoming attitude toward migration mixed with periods of greater restriction. The legal historian Aristide Zolberg notes that U.S. society's commitment to the social contract—the Enlightenment idea that government was a compact between individual citizens and the state—made citizenship something one could choose, not simply inherit. For most of the nation's history, however, the resulting welcome extended mainly to white Europeans. The first federal immigration law, passed in 1790, allowed for immigrants to become citizens after two years of residency (changed to five years in 1801, after a few years when it was fourteen), but only white, free persons of "satisfactory character" qualified. That consensus held despite passage of the Fourteenth Amendment to the Constitution, which eliminated restrictions on those in slavery or servitude and those with African ancestry. Asians remained ineligible.[17]

With these few exceptions, for most of the nineteenth century, immigration was actually managed not by federal laws but by state laws, as well as by laws and regulations around travel and commerce. This combination of legal structures led to "remote control," where entry was restricted at ports of embarkation, at different junctures preventing those who were indigent, sick, convicts, or politically suspect from getting on ships to immigrate. Later those restrictions were enforced on the U.S. side, at immigration stations like Ellis Island in New York or Angel Island in San Francisco. Mostly forgotten today is how the *emigration*, that is, departure of African Americans was encouraged by the U.S. government's establishment of a colony in West Africa for freed slaves, the nation now known as Liberia.[18]

Immigration from Asia really began in the mid-nineteenth century as the result of deliberate government policy, as Secretary of State William H. Steward, for example, negotiated various treaties with Asian governments to allow the recruitment of laborers to work on the transcontinental railroad and other projects. This, Zolberg notes, was the beginning of a tradition of the U.S. government making use of international agreements to help businesses secure cheaper labor.[19] Especially in the West, a potent combination of labor and racial unrest among white immigrants led to a series of measures against Asian immigrants, beginning in the 1870s with laws restricting female immigrants from China, continuing with the infamous Chinese Exclusion Acts of the 1880s, and leading to various laws and agreements that restricted the entry of Japanese, Korean, and finally Filipino migrants. Attempts to restrict the citizenship of the Chinese American descendants of immigrants, however, ran afoul of the Fourteenth Amendment, which granted citizenship to all persons born in the United States, the so-called *jus soli* principle, the "law of the soil." The gradual restrictions aimed at Asians also had the effect of encouraging the contracting of agricultural laborers from Mexico in the late nineteenth and early twentieth centuries.[20]

As immigration from Europe to the United States shifted south and east in origin during the last decades of the nineteenth century, a new burst of nativism arrived on the scene targeting Italians, Eastern European Jews, and Catholics, as well as Asian immigrants. The rise of "scientific racism," racist attitudes endorsed by intellectuals and eugenicists and supported by dubious scientific studies, gave overt racial prejudice a pseudo-empirical glow. Various restrictionist measures were proposed and many passed. By the 1920s, postwar isolationism pushed white Americans toward a greater embrace of immigrant restriction, and in 1924 Congress passed the Reed-Johnson Act, enshrining in law a quota system initially rooted in the percentage of various national groups according to the 1890 census but fine-tuned during the 1920s so that it favored immigrants from Western Europe.[21] Asian immigrants were barred entirely. The quota system reduced immigration dramatically. It also had unintended consequences, including temporarily strengthening Mexican immigration to the United States, since the law set no quotas for the Western hemisphere; bolstering the Great Migration of African American workers to the North to offset labor shortages; and, tragically, allowing for the exclusion of Jewish refugees from Eastern Europe, condemning many of those whose ships were sent away to death in the concentration camps.

Immigration remained much lower for the next five decades. During the 1930s, the global impact of the Great Depression also kept migration low, with its effects on market forces and government policies. While Mexican migration to the United States, for example, spiked during the 1920s, the restrictionist spirit of the era led to the creation of the Border Patrol, which eventually made prodigious use of inspections at ports of entry to regulate migration from Latin America. During the Depression, as job worries grew among whites, the U.S. government and local authorities deported or applied pressure for the "voluntary" departure of hundreds of thousands of Mexicans, who took their U.S.-citizen family members with them. The mid-twentieth century also brought a sustained push toward assimilation by American institutions of all kinds—government, schools, churches—creating a dominant white culture that was less exclusively associated with Anglo-Saxon

Protestantism. The Second World War helped that process along, as whites of all ethnicities fought together, and it finally ignited the U.S. economy to life, even as its mobilization of young men led to the creation of the contract worker *bracero* program with the government of Mexico. That same war also began to demonstrate the ethnic and racial bias embedded in the immigration quota system, as persons from Allied nations in Asia (e.g., nationalist China) were explicitly barred from entry. The mistreatment of nonwhite soldiers, who had served with distinction in segregated units, helped to spark both the Civil Rights Movement of the 1950s and 1960s and a host of ethnic rights movements in the late 1960s and 1970s.

In the end, many factors, including the horrors of Jewish refugee rejection during the *Shoah*, or Holocaust, the embarrassment of excluding persons from Allied nations, and the Jim Crow oppression brought to light by the Civil Rights Movements, shone a light on the explicit racial and ethnic prejudice embedded in the 1920s quotas. During the 1940s and 1950s, Asian exclusion was gradually rescinded, and allowance was made for refugees from Europe. In 1965, Congress passed a more complete reform of immigration law, the Hart-Celler Act. This law established the basic structure of contemporary immigration policy. It designated an overall cap for immigration visas, which was subsequently increased, prioritizing family reunification and professional skills, with precise quotas and classifications for each. It eliminated national quotas but set limits on the number of visas any nation could have, currently no more than 7 percent of all visas. The 7 percent limit was meant to atone for prejudicial quotas, but it had the unforeseen effect of creating bottlenecks of years or even decades for sending countries with large numbers of applicants, today including Mexico, India, the Philippines, and China among others. Its precision made little to no space for nonprofessional migrants without family in the United States. Both the bottleneck and the lack of a pathway for service workers, coupled with a robust economic demand for such workers, has facilitated the sustained flow of unauthorized immigrants, more than half who overstay a visitor's visa, and another half who cross the border without papers.

Subsequent federal immigration laws mostly amended the 1965 law, initially to accommodate refugees. The 1965 law had created a small number of visas for refugees, but the proxy conflicts of the Cold War created a kind of sustained attention to their plight. In 1966, provision was made for almost unlimited Cuban refugees, and the Refugee Act of 1980 passed in response to Vietnamese refugee resettlement during the late 1970s, though legally it was a comprehensive response to the United Nations Convention Relating to the Status of Refugees of 1951. Other post-1965 immigration laws included the 1986 Immigration and Control Act (IRCA) signed by President Ronald Reagan, a Solomonic combination of (1) hiring procedures and employer sanctions designed to prevent the employment of unauthorized immigrants and (2) amnesty provisions for unauthorized immigrants already in the country for several years. A 1990 law established a "diversity" lottery to encourage migration from nations who send few migrants to the United States, and in 1996, President Bill Clinton signed the Illegal Immigration Reform and Immigrant Responsibility Act. This law expedited removal proceedings, created a long list of deportable criminal offenses, including many misdemeanors, banned the extension of government benefits to unauthorized immigrants, limited the government benefits immigrants entering legally could receive, and funded the creation of border fences along the southern border. Congressional bottlenecks have prevented any sort of comprehensive immigration laws since then. This in part inspired President Barack Obama to defer indefinitely the deportation of many unauthorized immigrants who arrived as young children, popularly known as "Dreamers," the program known as Deferred Action for Childhood Arrivals (DACA).

REASONS PEOPLE UPROOT THEIR LIVES

At the beginning of this chapter, I noted that most people in the world do not migrate. While the people of wealthier receiving nations like Canada or the United States may assume that every person in poorer sending nations would come if they could, in fact most people do not want to migrate. To migrate is to uproot one's entire life, to leave behind beloved family members and familiar places, to struggle to succeed in an unfamiliar culture where at least some people would have preferred that you had not come. When I visited the families and neighbors of Mexican immigrants from the U.S. Midwest in Mexico in 2008, I encountered a great number of people with no desire to come to the United States and a few who had come and then left because they did not find it particularly hospitable. Visiting the Dominican Republic back in 1997, I met a schoolteacher with something resembling contempt for men he knew who left their wives and children behind to try and earn money in New York City. By the time I visited the Dominican Republic again twenty years later, the economy was much better, and many fewer people wanted to migrate.

There is another underappreciated reason why many people never even consider migration as an option—they are too poor. Migration requires at least some resources: to pay for a passport and visa, book travel, hire a smuggler, and purchase the basics for an entirely new household in a foreign land. Despite deeply held cultural narratives about "poor, huddled masses longing to be free" (see the next chapter), in truth the desperately poor do not migrate because they cannot afford to do so. Nor do they possess the necessary information about how to go about migrating or the interpersonal networks that help them know where to go. Those who migrate usually have at least some resources or relatives with such, a few connections, and some education. As sociologists Alejandro Portes and Rubén Rumbaut note, "The flow coming to the United States, in particular, does not originate mostly in the poorest countries or the most destitute regions….Even those from the most modest regions—for instance, [undocumented] labor migrants from Mexico and Central America—tend to have educational levels that are higher on average than their respective sending populations."[22] In wealthier countries where public education is ubiquitous, we easily forget that money for uniforms, books, and travel to school may inhibit the poorest from acquiring much education.

For those who are not desperately poor, no one can point to a single reason or cultural narrative to explain why people migrate. I met a man in the state of Puebla in Mexico who told me that he went to the United States because his university education was not sufficient to gain professional work; you needed to have connections to power brokers, which he did not have. The parents of one young migrant told me that from a very young age all he talked about was going to the United States; it was his dream. A Colombian told me he left because he fell in love with an American man. A colleague of mine came to the United States because she could not pursue a doctorate in theology in her native country in Asia. A former professor of mine found the German educational system a little too strict and hierarchical to make space for her to become the kind of educator she hoped to be. Some go

36

on the move to escape political or religious persecution, others to attain greater economic opportunities, not a few to live in a more accepting environment for nontraditional gender roles or LGBT identity. Some people simply cannot say why they came. Given the divergent personal explanations, it should perhaps surprise no one that social scientists do not agree on what impels people to migrate.

Traditionally, economists spoke of "push" and "pull" factors driving an individual's cost-benefit analysis of migration as an economic option. The classic scenario was of a young man surveying conditions of underemployment or low pay in his hometown, while he hears of more or better job opportunities elsewhere. My story of the Mexican college graduate unable to get work in his field partially fits this pattern. Today, however, economists and other social scientists argue that the decision to go most frequently occurs not at the level of the individual, but at the household level. Organized crime gangs in some Central American cities, for example, have become so violent that families see their teenage or young adult children's dangerous journey north with smugglers as safer than staying, where the only options appear to be joining or being marked for death by a criminal gang. Even in less dramatic situations, a household may find that migration offers a workable strategy to address what social scientists call *relative deprivation*, that is, the felt sense that one remains poor in comparison to the economic status of others.[23]

In real life, of course, the decision to migrate may not always have a rational basis clearly tied to some cost-benefit analysis. Recall the man who fell in love or the young man who from a young age dreamed of coming to the United States. The mother of the latter showed me a portrait taken several years ago, long before he ever set foot in the United States. He smiles broadly for the mall photographer, an American flag in the background. Even more problematic is the way this kind of rational choice analysis, whether at the individual or household level, leaves out larger social, economic, and political factors that shape where and when people go. Some social scientists point to today's hourglass economy, with its large swaths of jobs for professionals or management workers at the top and unskilled service workers at the bottom, working in restaurants or hospitality, for example. Middle-level manufacturing jobs or highly skilled work have shrunk considerably. In many cases, native-born workers refuse to take low-paying service jobs, creating a robust job market for immigrants, who often still earn more than they would at home, even without legal status.[24]

Even putting such trends in the global economy aside, the specific destination of an immigrant is often shaped by the historical ties between nations, especially those forged through political or economic colonization. Jamaicans, for example, have migrated in large numbers to Great Britain in part because of the things that came with British colonization—the English language, a familiarity with British political and economic institutions. For similar reasons, many Moroccans and Algerians migrated to France. Americans move to Mexico in part inspired by experiences there as tourists. U.S. political and military support for the Republic of South Vietnam in the 1950s and 1960s factored both in the decision of the U.S. government to shelter Vietnamese refugees when South Vietnam fell and in the decision of refugees to seek asylum in the United States. Some political theorists go beyond these specific relationships to envision the entire global economy as an asymmetrical capitalist system where wealthy countries accumulate capital and poorer countries supply labor and materials, including labor moved to the affluent nation through migration.[25]

Though these different economic explanations may tell us something about why people decide to migrate and to where, they do not tell us much about the mechanics of the process of migration. How do people learn about the destinations where they eventually move? How do they connect to work opportunities or to communities of people from home? For those able to obtain a visa, how do they manage to navigate that process effectively? For those who cross the border, how do they know where to go to secure a smuggler and how much to pay that smuggler? In short, how do people know *how* to migrate? The answer is that they make use of interpersonal networks. Through these networks, migrants find out not only about the demand for their work but also whether or not the circumstances of that work are desirable.[26] The networks may start with extended family, derided as *chain migration* by opponents of immigration, but they grow as the migrant journeys on and encounters others along the way:

> Migrants also rely on informal trust relationships to minimize the risks associated with moving to a foreign land. These contacts with friends, families and employers provide an important means through which immigrants gain and

accumulate social capital. By social capital we mean the repertoire of resources such as information, material assistance, and social support that flow through ties to kin, community, and institutions — churches, for example.[27]

Doing research in a particular Midwestern city, I learned that all the migrants living in a trailer park in town were from the same city in the Mexican state of Puebla. Not only had word spread in Puebla about the job opportunities, new arrivals were assisted and guided toward housing in the same trailer park. In a different part of Mexico, I met the brother of a Mexican immigrant I had come to know well, and the brother explained to me how he had preceded my friend and then communicated back to him about the possibilities. Such networks also facilitate the movement of internal migrants. During the mid-twentieth century, African Americans in the South found out about work opportunities in northern cities through other people from their towns and villages who had already made the move. My own parents ended up in a particular city in the Los Angeles area because of information provided by my mother's uncle and my grandmother.

The kinds of networks a migrant might engage depend on a migrant's resources and goals, that is, what "migration trajectory" they are following. I have known immigrants who came to work in factories, others who ended up as house cleaners, some doctors and nurses, a few engineers, a taxi driver who had been a professor, and several who hoped from the beginning to build up businesses. Portes and Rumbaut argue that there are essentially four distinct migration trajectories, those of the following types of people: (1) labor migrants, such as farmworkers, manual laborers, and low-pay service workers like busboys and home health aides; (2) professional migrants, including doctors and nurses, engineers and those in the technology industry, professors; (3) entrepreneurial migrants, including those who create small businesses like groceries, dry cleaners, nail salons, donut shops, construction firms, and restaurants, often but not always located in ethnic enclaves; and (4) refugees and asylees, who are admitted to a receiving country because they have a well-founded fear of persecution because of a group they belong to back home, whether that group is a political or religious organization or a persecuted minority group.[28]

Each of these types brings particular advantages and challenges in terms of the kind of reception they receive in the community to which they move. "For immigrants, the most relevant contexts of reception are defined by the policies of the receiving governments, the conditions of the host labor market, and the characteristics of their own ethnic communities."[29] Though there are unauthorized migrants of each migrant type, labor migrants are much more likely to be undocumented. While the demand for their work is often robust, there are few legal avenues for them to enter the United States. Their work often saddles them with low social status; they can become invisible and subject to abuse with little recourse. My students and I, for example, have had the opportunity to chat with day laborers outside a Home Depot store. They told us multiple stories about working a day or even several days at hard labor, only to have the recruiter disappear without paying them or even without transporting them home. A friend told me about working in the fields as a teenager and how the employer would himself call immigration authorities just before payday.

Professional migrants, on the other hand, may have a much easier time procuring a visa, usually through the sponsorship of a company who employs them. This is often true of science and technology workers, but it is also true of, for example, Catholic priests recruited by a bishop to compensate for the U.S. priest shortage. While professional migrants tend to be remunerated well, they generally have to begin again at the foundation levels of their fields.[30] Thus, my dental hygienist when I lived in New York City was formerly a dentist back in her native Colombia. Professional migrants may also be vulnerable to mistreatment, even sexual harassment, from their employers, on whose good graces they depend to maintain their immigration status. Entrepreneurial migrants, on the other hand, often arrive legally via family reunification visas, though wealthier entrepreneurs do receive "employment creating" visas by investing significant capital, usually several hundred thousand dollars.[31]

ASSIMILATION ANXIETIES

Whatever the economic trajectory of migrants, whatever resources they do or do not bring, migrants find that they need to adapt in some way to their new home. How quickly they adapt, and according to whose terms, often proves the most contentious aspect of migration, both from the migrant perspective and that of the receiving community. Conflicts and tensions emerge all the time. A parent volunteer instructs a student not to speak Spanish at recess to another child, even though that child arrived from Mexico days before. Parents press to have religious instruction in their home languages, even as the young people prefer English, or in other cases long for a bilingual experience. Sometimes the tensions remain internal to immigrants or their children. A college student from an immigrant family worries that her white peers will not accept her but also wonders whether all this time in a "white dominant institution" will change her unrecognizably.

Such mixed feelings about adopting elements of the receiving culture are far from new. For much of the nineteenth century, European immigrants fought over how much and how quickly they should adopt U.S. customs and mores, with Germans often advocating for slower adaptation and (Catholic) Irish for more rapid "Americanization." Even as the immigrants themselves fought over this question, the receiving community of "mainstream" Americans, which in that era were white Protestant Americans of British heritage, also argued about it. Thus, despite their eagerness to adapt, the Catholic Irish were often identified by white Protestant Americans as so ethnically and religiously *other*—unrefined in appearance, violent, corrupt, prone to drink—that adaptation to American ways appeared unimaginable. In our own time, complaints from receiving communities about immigrant adaptation often center on immigrants' alleged unwillingness to learn English. Ironically, as noted in the previous chapter, more of today's recent immigrants speak English than did their counterparts in the early twentieth century.[32]

Worries about immigrant adaptation on the part of a receiving community may come across as reasonable questions about how to hold on to national unity as migrants bring their differing customs. The late political scientist Samuel Huntington, for example, wrote a book near the end of his life in which he argued that an influx of Latin American immigrants, unwilling to assimilate, threatened a national consensus over the "core culture" of the United States, which he rather explicitly associated not only with democracy but also with Protestantism and Anglo-Saxon culture.[33] After publication, more than a few critics drew attention to flaws in the reasoning, including inaccuracies about the degree to which Latinx Americans actually assimilate, and they wondered if Huntington's personal fears and white Protestant ethnocentrism had clouded his judgment.[34]

While there are reasonable arguments to make about what adaptation is required of immigrants for practical reasons, much of the worries about immigrant adaptation seem fueled by deep emotional reactions or resistance. Recall the rather nasty tone of Benjamin Franklin's complaints about German immigrants, which seem to center on customs that he found personally distasteful. Intercultural communication theorists argue that encounters with persons from a different culture often engender uncertainty and anxiety. In the midst of such encounters, it becomes uncomfortably clear that our customary cultural rules for everyday interaction do not apply. We quite literally do not know what we are doing.[35] I can remember launching into a spirited American-style argument over some facts of Mexican history at a dinner party in Mexico City, only to realize by the silence that ensued that I had committed a major social faux pas. The shame of having embarrassed myself and my host kept me silent for the rest of the evening. In the context of immigration, uncertainty and anxiety occur in one's own land, adding a kind of grief to the mix, grief that one's community has been irrevocably changed by newcomers. An understandable though irrational reaction, then, is to want newcomers to adapt rapidly. But such adaptation, as we will see below, is considerably more complicated than most receiving community members realize. Yet, when it does not occur at the expected rapid pace, complaints inevitably arise that migrant neighbors are unwilling to adapt. In the next chapter, we will see how one of the persistent cultural narratives around immigration in American life is that migrants will not or cannot truly "become American," though it is often unclear what this actually means.

More disturbing, this kind of discomfort and impatience takes on even greater intensity as it is coupled with ethnic, religious, and racial prejudices and stereotypes. Thus, Chinese immigrants in the post–Gold Rush era were termed "unassimilable" and eventually excluded, not ultimately because their appearance, food, or customs "felt" different—no doubt they did—but because these differences became emblematic of widespread racial stereotypes of Chinese immigrants as pagan, inscrutable, dishonest, and dirty. More recently, I have heard arguments against immigration that seem to depend on dizzyingly contrary stereotypes of Mexicans, that they are both lazy—taking

42

advantage of social services they have not worked for—and so inhumanly industrious that they steal American jobs. We should be clear that, despite the prevalence and influence of nativist prejudice and discrimination across history, there have always been members of receiving communities who vociferously objected to such characterizations. At the height of anti-Chinese sentiment in the 1880s, a cartoonist for a popular newspaper created a cartoon portraying a Chinese man sitting outside the closed "Golden Gate of Liberty," his belongings sprawled around him, each a box or bag with a label disputing anti-Chinese stereotypes: "order," "sobriety," "peace," and "industry."[36] In my own research, I ran into more than one white Catholic who was more than ready to welcome newcomers from Latin America, one elderly volunteer commenting simply, "Well, if you can't speak English, well then, that's fine."[37]

STUDYING IMMIGRANT ADAPTATION

Whether greeted with suspicion or welcome, the process of immigrant adaptation is real and complex, but it is also often not well understood. The first influential social scientific studies of immigrant adaptation in the United States took place under Robert Park and other sociologists at the University of Chicago beginning in the 1920s. These scholars began to refer to the process of immigrant adaptation as *assimilation*, a word whose origins in English refer to absorption of nutrients into the body.[38] Park and his colleagues saw assimilation as an irreversible "process of interpenetration and fusion" by which distinct immigrants and immigrant groups were incorporated into "a common cultural life."[39] Even as government, churches, and other institutions of the time pushed migrants to rapidly adopt the dominant Anglo-Protestant culture and customs, the Chicago sociologists observed that assimilation moved slowly, working its way through competition between ethnic groups into mutual accommodation. It had limits. Drawing on their studies of still vibrant immigrant communities in Chicago, then an immigrant-majority city, they assumed that assimilation would also change the dominant culture over time.[40]

The most influential understanding of assimilation, however, arrived in a different era, during the 1960s when the foreign-born population of the United States crept toward a low not seen since the early days of the Republic. Sociologist Milton Gordon saw assimilation as an inevitable, multidimensional process by which immigrants and immigrant groups gradually abandon almost all of the cultural heritage of their ancestors and adopt the "core culture" of the United States, which Gordon saw as middle class, white, Protestant, and largely traceable to British origins. With one eye on the decline of European ethnicity in postwar America, Gordon and colleagues like him saw assimilation as a near linear progression toward intermarriage and a strong sense of identifying with the dominant culture. This view appeared to be in accord with the Americanization push of the first half of the twentieth century, and it has shown a certain durability in the popular imagination, especially among the thoroughly assimilated descendants of European immigrants.[41]

It fell out of favor among scholars, however, by the 1970s and 1980s. This "canonical" view of assimilation privileged a European and white experience of immigration, one marked by decades of immigration restriction. After 1965, of course, Latin American and Asian source nations dominated migration to the United States, and this account of assimilation did not seem tailored to them. The Civil Rights Movement of the 1950s and 1960s and the racial and ethnic pride movements of the late 1960s into the 1970s demanded a more expansive and inclusive notion of American nationality, one that made more space for African Americans and people of Latin American ancestry, Asian Americans, American Indians, and immigrants from everywhere *besides* Europe. White supremacy had not vanished, but it could no longer function as an unquestioned assumption of U.S. national identity, even among white people. Accordingly, notions of assimilation focused on "Anglo conformity" began to look more transparently coercive, narrow, and racially prejudicial. Could not nonwhite immigrants and their families legitimately hold on to aspects of their home cultures even as they adapted to life in the United States?[42]

Sociologists began to speak of *segmented assimilation*, wherein immigrants and their U.S.-born children would adapt not to an amorphous Anglo-dominant American culture but to specific segments within American society, often segments segregated by socioeconomic class, race, ethnicity, or region. Indeed, when I worked in Harlem in New York City, I did not see the darker-skinned children of immigrants from the Dominican Republic in the Caribbean becoming "mainstream

Americans." They assimilated to the working class African American culture dominant in the area. Mexican immigrants in Texas's Rio Grande Valley do not adapt to Euro-American ways; they adopt Mexican American Tejano ways. The children of upper middle-class English immigrants in Southern California are most likely to resemble other affluent white Southern Californians. Sociologists point out that all of these are American cultures, but they are not all alike. The evidence of studies of more recent migration, they argue, suggests that a host of factors shape what kind of societal segment one assimilates to. These include (1) job skills, education, work experience, English-language facility, and wealth, collectively known as *human capital*; (2) migration conditions upon arrival including immigration status, the welcome or discrimination they might face from receiving communities, and government resources they do or do not have access to; (3) the presence or absence and social status of a community of immigrants with similar origins; and (4) family structures, especially whether an immigrant family is headed by one or two parents, and to a lesser extent, the presence or absence of an extended family.[43]

For example, a nurse from the Philippines who came to the United States during nursing shortages of the 1990s and early 2000s came with relatively high human capital—education, English-language facility, and badly needed job skills. He or she had access to a professional visa process and probably joined a vibrant immigrant community if the workplace was in a major American city. If it was on the West Coast, then the nurse may also have had relatives nearby. None of this means an immigrant nurse would not encounter prejudice or discrimination. I myself have overheard pejorative stereotypes of Filipinos as insular or dishonest bandied about, and they have a disturbing similarity to age-old anti-Asian tropes. Nevertheless, such a person is much more likely to find himself or herself part of a middle-class, educated community of Filipino Americans, or perhaps intermarried into another relatively affluent group. On the other hand, a Central American working-class family whose parents lack education or legal status will likely find themselves adapting to an urban working-class community, perhaps Spanish speaking or bilingual, even if the children learn English in public schools. The presence of large numbers of similarly situated conationals may make it easier to find a job. In other cases, such neighborhoods may lack jobs, especially jobs that pay the rent or lead to social mobility. Education can come to feel useless. The most dangerous outcome in such a situation is that young people assimilate to a criminal segment by joining a gang. Social scientists sometimes describe this as "downward assimilation."[44]

The sociologist Tomás Jiménez focuses on this process of segmented assimilation in a more specific way. Taking the case of persons of Mexican ancestry, Jiménez argues for the importance of *continuing* migration for the formation of ethnic identity among the descendants of immigrants, what he calls "immigrant replenishment." "Immigration is perhaps *the* defining event in the Mexican-American narrative, because it is both a past and present event."[45] As noted above, earlier more linear and irrevocable views of assimilation emerged out of the experience of European immigrants during an era of restriction. Throughout much of the twentieth century, people of Irish or Italian ancestry were unlikely to encounter recent immigrants from those lands, and their connection to their ancestry became more a matter of choosing baby names, listening to popular music by Italian American artists, or wearing green on St. Patrick's Day.

But Jiménez argues that even Mexican Americans of the third or fourth generation, who may not speak Spanish at all, cannot escape seeing their own identity as shaped by people still arriving. "Immigrant replenishment thus makes ethnicity less symbolic, less optional, and more consequential for all members of the replenished group."[46] In the case of Mexican Americans, the size of the "replenishing" group at 28 percent of all immigrants[47] multiplies this impact. On the one hand, Mexican culture remains abundantly and joyfully present, even outside of the traditional gateway cities of the Southwest. On the other hand, the larger proportion of poor service workers and unauthorized immigrants among recent arrivals can stigmatize Mexican identity, an impact seen clearly in the anti-Mexican rhetoric of the Trump administration.[48] This can lead to increased solidarity, as when Mexican American voters turned California politics resoundingly Democrat after a state initiative supported by Republicans targeted undocumented immigrants. It can also lead to distancing, as when the cofounder of Latinos for Trump said during the 2016 election, "My culture is a very dominant culture, and it's imposing and it's causing problems. If you don't do something about it, you're going to have taco trucks on every corner."[49]

Jiménez has also spent significant time studying regions with high immigrant density, like Silicon Valley in Northern California, and he shows how migration also changes the cultural patterns and expectations of receiving communities:

> Assimilation is relational: it involves back-and-forth adjustments in daily life by both newcomers and established individuals as they come in contact with one another....When considered side by side, the processes of established and newcomer adjustment are mirror images: both parties feel a tremendous sense of loss, often longing for the way things were; both also feel a sense of gain because of the dynamism that migration can produce. But the deliberate and incidental adjustments that established and newcomer individuals make are more than just mirror images—they implicate one another...newcomers' efforts to maintain a cultural connection to their country of origin through language, food, and religious customs led established individuals to conceive of a more expansive notion of cultural norms and their own relationship to those norms.[50]

My own life in Los Angeles witnesses to the truth of this. For my wife and me, tacos are comfort food we grew up with. This last year I sent out a greeting to all of our department's graduate students on the occasion of lunar new year in early February, and one of my classes celebrated the holiday with a Vietnamese nun by eating traditional candies. An older priest I know of mixed Portuguese and Hawaiian heritage hands out red envelopes to younger people according to Chinese custom for the holiday. And my deferential respect for elderly people emerged not from my own family experience but from my years working in the Mexican community. Especially in immigrant-rich areas, assimilation is a two-sided process, even if the adaptations are not of equal intensity.

Finally, a few scholars have noted how the adaptation of immigrants also leads to a process of change in sending communities. Some of these changes have to do with remittances (money sent home by migrants) and economic investment by migrants who return. The sociologist Peggy Levitt describes how Gujarati migrants from northwestern India supported families, built schools, and renovated houses across the towns they came from.[51] I myself witnessed a beautiful town square and church in a central Mexican town, both renovated by money sent from the Midwestern United States. And influence on sending communities is cultural as well as financial, sometimes described as *social remittances*. Levitt presents a Pakistani tech worker who lived in the United States talking about how transnational conversations have brought at least some American work culture habits to the tech sector in Pakistan.[52] In 2018, a *New York Times* article and accompanying photographs showed a Guatemalan town transformed by the migration of its inhabitants to the United States. American flags adorned many tombs in the local cemetery, and among the corrugated tin and cinder block houses were larger homes built in styles of architecture common in the United States, at least one in colonial revival style built by a man who had cleaned such houses in the New York City area.[53]

FACTS AND NARRATIVES

The preceding examination of immigrant adaptation dispels any notion of "assimilation" working as a clear, rapid, linear process. Migrants adapt gradually, usually to a segment within U.S. society. Many factors shape the process of adaptation, including the skills and education they bring with them and the discrimination or acceptance they face upon arrival. We saw how migration forges changes in receiving and sending communities. This chapter also examined the complex reasons that drive people to migrate. Before that, we looked at the multilayered history of migration to North America, as well as how it shaped and was shaped by immigration laws. These are the elements of an "empirical narrative about migration," that is, a more data-driven account of migrants, the communities who receive them, and those who remain in the communities who send them. Hopefully, this account allows us to deepen our understanding of migration, to develop empathy for people on all sides of it, and to contest too simplistic explanations. Yet, as the introduction demonstrated, the cultural narratives that members of receiving communities have inherited often have the emotional feel of truth, even if they do not reflect the facts and evidence-based conclusions reported in this chapter. What are those stories? Why do they have such a hold on us? We turn to such cultural narratives in the next chapter.

Section Two

CULTURAL NARRATIVES AND MIGRATION

Here at our sea-washed, sunset gates shall stand
A mighty woman with a torch, whose flame
Is the imprisoned lightning, and her name
Mother of Exiles. From her beacon-hand
Glows worldwide welcome…
"Give me your tired, your poor,
Your huddled masses yearning to breathe free,
The wretched refuse of your teeming shore.
Send these, the homeless, tempest-tost to me,
I lift my lamp beside the golden door!"

—Emma Lazarus, from "The New Colossus"

The average Catholic Irishman of the first generation as represented in this Assembly, is a low, venal, corrupt, and unintelligent brute.

—Theodore Roosevelt[1]

Then my dad got into a car crash where he broke his jaw, and they had to borrow money from my father's family, who are bad, greedy people. The idea of coming to America to work for a year to make just enough money to pay off the debt came up and it seemed like a good idea.

—Karla Cornejo Villavicencio[2]

Chapter Three

AMERICAN DREAMS AND NIGHTMARES

Migration According to Receiving Communities

Not long ago I conducted a summer independent study course on immigration for one of our students, a young woman about to finish our graduate program before she went off to doctoral studies abroad. Influenced by the advocacy for undocumented students of one of my colleagues, and the daughter of an immigrant herself, she became something of an immigration activist. I could not have imagined a more enthusiastic student of the subject. To begin, we read some sociological research on immigration together. One of the sources argued a point I mentioned in the previous chapter of this book, that in general the poorest of the poor do not migrate. In a way I did not expect, that simple fact shook her. On the one hand, she accepted both the logic of this conclusion that very destitute people have no resources to move at all and that it was rooted in extensive research. On the other hand, she had internalized a cultural narrative about migration that saw deep poverty and great deprivation as its prime motivator, especially for those who cross the border without papers. In her activism work, she had persistently argued that extreme poverty justified whatever steps families felt they had to take outside the law. I assured her that there were other, even better reasons why unauthorized immigrants deserved a break, and I admitted that many migrants, especially those who cross the border without papers, are indeed poor, even if not destitute. Still, she continued to look disturbed.

Later it occurred to me that our conversation had touched something deep in her, a cultural narrative about migration that had a strong claim on her. Indeed, in the introduction, we saw the power of such narratives on how we imagine the world. Having heard them repeatedly, we *feel* that they tell us something essential and important about how things are, about who *we* are, and about how things ought to be. My student had repeatedly heard that unauthorized immigrants come to escape the effects of extreme deprivation on their families, and as a cultural narrative it certainly sounded like a compelling account of reality. But that story also touched on her own identity, both as a deeply empathetic person who cares about those who suffer, which she truly is, and as the child of an immigrant. Indeed, the descendants of immigrants, even those removed by generations, cannot help but look for their own family stories in the cultural narratives about migration they hear. The narrative also reminded her of her hope for a better world, one where poor children did not starve simply because they were born on the wrong side of a border.

When a cultural narrative performs in that way—offers a story of how things are, who we are, and how things ought to be—it is not so easy to dispense with, even when plain facts contradict it. For example, another widely shared cultural narrative about unauthorized immigrants is that they come to occupy jobs that otherwise would be held by the U.S. born, or in the more common parlance, "They take our jobs." Yet, by and large, undocumented immigrants do not compete with U.S.-born people for jobs they find and some evidence suggests that their presence may even create jobs for native-born Americans.[3] Nevertheless, the "stealing our jobs" narrative *feels* to many like an accurate account of reality, perhaps especially when local jobs do not seem plentiful or have been "outsourced" to other countries. It also touches on identity: few Americans would want to think of themselves as people who let outsiders take something that belongs to them. Finally, it speaks to a vision of the country attractive to many people, where the U.S. born should have first right to the benefits of American life.

Upon cross-examination, both of these cultural narratives prove somewhat inaccurate in reality. But even inaccurate cultural narratives can contain pieces of truth. My student was not entirely wrong; people do come to the United States hoping for much better economic circumstances than they experienced back home, even if they were not starving there. And regarding the "steal our jobs" narrative, while it may be true that most immigrants—unauthorized or not—rarely replace citizens in a job market, there definitely exist sectors of the country where reliable middle-class jobs have vanished, including places with a lot of immigrants. In both of these cases, however, these pieces of truth get sensationalized to such a degree as to make the actual truth unrecognizable. This is not new. The anti-Chinese narratives of the late nineteenth century did tap into the considerable and baffling differences between Chinese and American cultures and the difficulty of understanding those differences. But that important fact became hopelessly lost amid a barrage of racial stereotypes about Chinese workers as deceitful and inscrutable. Cultural narratives also sensationalize by addressing very particular groups of people while leaving large groups of others out. Even the lovely description of the United States as a "nation of immigrants" is a cultural narrative without much appeal in the African American community, since African slaves did not come to this country as "immigrants." From the perspective of the descendants of African slaves, we might more plausibly envision the United States as a nation of kidnappers and hostages!

True or not, cultural narratives have power. The purpose of this chapter is to wrestle with three dominant cultural narratives among receiving communities in the United States. Many U.S. receiving communities are largely composed of the descendants of immigrants or internal migrants, which as we will see is not irrelevant to understanding the relationship between these narratives and memory. As we learned in the introductory chapter, both what some of us have forgotten about our own migration stories (amnesia) and rosy visions of those stories (nostalgia) may go a long way in explaining how cultural narratives emerge and what makes them compelling. The activist and New Testament scholar Ched Myers is more blunt: "Antipathy or even ambivalence toward immigrants and refugees indicates at best a profound suppression of our own past, at worst a deep, collective self-contempt."[4] When those of us from receiving communities no longer have a grasp of the complex, ambiguous, and difficult stories of our immigrant forebears, we find it a simple matter to buy into cultural narratives about migration that distort the truth. We do not look too deeply at what cultural narratives imply about how things are (reality), who Americans are (identity), and how the world ought to be (ethics). In the rest of this chapter, however, we will do just that, look deeply at the three important cultural narratives to see how their accounts of reality, identity, and ethics stack up. We will carefully consider what does not correspond to the facts and also what about these stories has troubling consequences or raises troubling implications.

Two of these narratives need little introduction. Ask almost anyone why people came or come to this country, and they will answer that they came or come seeking "a better life." As we will see, there are both political and economic versions of this American Dream story, but as a rule it remains central to Americans' sense of identity as a nation of immigrants, often propelled by a romanticizing immigrant nostalgia. We find it tied to the nation's most famous piece of public art, the Statue of Liberty in New York Harbor, with Emma Lazarus's famous poem, "The New Colossus," cast in bronze inside its base: "Give me your tired, your poor/Your huddled masses yearning to breathe free." The second famous cultural narrative casts immigrants not as pursuing a beautiful dream but as perpetuating a nightmare. Though this story perhaps remains less influential than the competing better life narrative, it creeps to the surface continually across U.S. history, construing immigrants as invaders, spoiling the American Dream for those who "belong" here, who are most frequently white. Indeed, this immigrant threat narrative often has racial or ethnic or religious overtones; its most famous targets were the Catholic Irish in the 1840s and 1850s, the Chinese and other East Asians in the last decades of the nineteenth century, and Latin Americans, especially Mexicans, or Muslims today.

The third important cultural narrative about immigration, summarized by reference to the "rule of law" and its contravention by unauthorized immigrants, sounds less like a dream or nightmare and more like a civics lesson. It posits a clear legal barrier dividing the good (legal) immigrants seeking a better life from the bad (illegal) immigrants who plunder or harm. In a way, it splits the difference between the previous two narratives. Controversy enters in, however, when the distinction between the two appears as much defined by race, ethnicity, or religion as it does by legal status. While the distinction between legal and illegal grows more complicated the more we know about immigration law and unauthorized migrants' stories, we underestimate the power of the "rule of law" narrative at our own peril. Finally, at the end of this chapter I will briefly consider a few other immigration narratives, less influential than the "big three."

AMERICAN DREAMS

The 2011 film *A Better Life* presents the tale of an undocumented immigrant and his U.S.-born son. Directed by Chris Weitz, whose other more famous credits include *About a Boy* and one of the *Twilight* films, the film is a kind of *bildungsroman*, or coming-of-age story. The American-born son is transformed as he becomes more acquainted with his undocumented immigrant father over the course of a day they spend together. The young man learns more about his father's struggles when young, his journey to the United States, and the sacrifices he has made for their family. In short, he begins to understand how he has a "better life" than his father did back in Mexico because of his father's willingness to cross the border without papers and work as a gardener. Even though the film focuses on an immigrant family, its intended audience does not appear to be immigrants, especially given its director's mainstream status, the frequent explanations of immigrant life (suggesting the viewer has little familiarity with them), and the language of most of the film: English. In short, this cinematic dramatization of the better life narrative was aimed not at immigrants but at receiving communities. Weitz said in an interview, "We don't really have a political agenda....It's simply that when you turn a camera on somebody, it's hard not to sympathize with them."[5]

The film presents an *economic* version of the better life narrative. Below we consider the political and religious version, focused on movement from persecution or oppression to freedom, but by far the more pervasive type of better life narrative is unrepentantly economic. The geographer William A.V. Clark notes, "The dream is and was unabashedly material....It is the same dream that propels so many new immigrants today, the dream of improving their lot, of doing better. Repeatedly, media anecdotes of immigrant success recount the sacrifices the first generation makes to ensure second-generation successes."[6] Clark and others point to the commonly understood indicators of a "better life," including a middle-class lifestyle, educational opportunities for children, and home ownership.[7]

Though it may in fact cultivate empathy with contemporary immigrant struggles, the economic better life narrative may ultimately have less to do with actual immigrants and more to do with the native-born's belief in or a disillusionment with the cultural narrative of the American Dream. Though the term was popularized by James Truslow Adams in 1931, in part to dispute the usefulness of Franklin Delano Roosevelt's New Deal government aid programs, the idea of the United States as a unique place where persons without resources can get ahead appears much earlier, most famously in the "rags-to-riches" stories associated with Horatio Alger's young adult novels across the nineteenth century. The sociologist Sandra Hanson and her political scientist coauthor, John Kenneth White, find the origins of the American Dream in the Declaration of Independence's proposal of a right to the pursuit of happiness, and they point to Alexis de Tocqueville's report in the 1830s on the link between material success and individualistic notions of self-reliance.[8]

Communications theorist Luke Winslow disputes this historical lineage, arguing that the popularity of the American Dream narrative is more the product of affluence following the Second World War and a turn in government rhetoric away from structural explanations for economic success or failure toward those highlighting individual ambition and grit. The term itself, he notes, rarely appears before the 1970s. Indeed, in the 1930s, James Truslow Adams's publisher would not let him title his book *The American Dream* because they thought no one would recognize the term.[9] Whatever the historical provenance, it seems clear that the cultural narrative of the American Dream does emphasize the role of individual drive and ambition in success rather than larger social forces like education or race and ethnicity or, for that matter, luck. Indeed, Clark emphasizes "the two elements that are threaded through the American Dream: a belief that there is a fair chance of succeeding and ample opportunities to do so. Everyone has a chance, the opportunities are there, and hard work will be rewarded."[10]

As nearly everyone acknowledges, of course, these presumptions of equal opportunity and fairness do not necessarily apply to all immigrants or all Americans. "Skills and opportunities are not always perfectly matched; constraints and discrimination in the system prevent some from achieving their dreams; sometimes skills cannot be transferred from other societies."[11] According to data from the World Bank, intergenerational social mobility in the United States is far below the global median, when measured by the number of people from the bottom half who make it to the top fourth. It is near the bottom when compared with other high-income countries.[12] In the mid-2000s, the economist George Borjas reviewed various studies of social mobility among immigrants and found that, on average, the children of immigrants did have better economic outcomes than their parents, and the grandchildren better than they. But stratification by ethnic group persisted across the generations. "In rough terms, about half of the differences in relative economic status across ethnic groups in one generation persist into the next."[13] This is to say that the children of poorer immigrant groups do move up, but more slowly than everyone else.

The sociologists Alejandro Portes and Rubén Rumbaut studied the family income of immigrants who had entered between 1970 and 1985 in the mid-1990s, that is, ten to twenty-five years after entry. They found Haitians and Mexicans earning less than almost everyone else and Europeans, Chinese, Filipinos, and Cubans earning more than everyone else. They found that more years in the United States, more English, more education, and professional status were associated with better economic outcomes. Even so, the uneven way different groups are received into the United States—for example, the refugee status afforded Cuban and Vietnamese versus the immigration barriers to Mexicans and Haitians—matters a great deal.[14] There is also some disturbing evidence that, for Mexican immigrants, economic outcomes improve between the immigrant generation and their children but then stagnate after that.[15] In short, for immigrant groups with less education, fewer resources, and facing more ethnic and racial discrimination, the "better life" is only a little better, and over the generations it may not be much better at all.

The better life economic narrative may not adequately represent the *reality*, that is, the uncertain economic progress of immigrants today, but it has a strong hold on the imagination of receiving communities. Part of the reason for this attachment is the way in which the better life narrative appears to offer a compelling account of their own intergenerational story, their *identity* as descendants of immigrants. Most families of European immigrant stock have now lived in the United States for four or more generations, and for some, many more. A majority, though not all, arrived in the middle class at least a generation ago, often as a result of the phenomenal postwar economic expansion between 1945 and 1970. In the 1920s, less than a third of the nation's families were middle class, but by the mid-1950s it was almost two-thirds.[16] But how long it took their ancestors to achieve that lifestyle, what poverty or discrimination they endured, all that remains lost in history. Most Americans today may not realize, for example, that before the Second World War less than half of families owned their own homes, for down payments were usually half of the home value and mortgages for a decade or less.[17] Thus, when Americans of European stock hold to a narrative of immigration that emphasizes a better economic life, they may be thinking more of their own families' experiences after the Second World War rather than the halting immigrant social mobility of both a century ago and today.

Even if the economic progress of a "better life" was in truth the unique result of particular twentieth-century economic realities, such as the Great Depression, the fast-paced industrial output of the war, and the economic growth of a victor whose infrastructure did not lie in ruins, it *feels* more compelling to imagine it is the inevitable result of a nation of industrious, capable individuals devoted to ever renewed economic process.[18] In this sense, the economic better life narrative taps into deeply held American *ethical* ideas about the value of hard work and self-reliance. In reality, of course, hard work and self-reliance go much further when they are accompanied by education, family stability, good connections, and a racial or ethnic identity the "mainstream" finds relatively unproblematic.

Some commentators rightly attest that the "better life" toward which people strive has never simply been a pursuit of material progress. People migrate looking for better political or religious circumstances, the opportunity to live one's beliefs without persecution by fellow citizens or the government. This political or religious version of the better life narrative echoes the "yearning to breathe free" sentiment of Emma Lazarus's poem, and it appears in political speeches given across U.S. history, including those by George Washington, Franklin Delano Roosevelt, and Ronald Reagan.[19] The narrative coheres with the consistent rhetoric of freedom and liberty in founding national documents like the Declaration of Independence and contemporary political speeches. The political-religious narrative took on greater resonance during the Cold War, when refugees from communist nations sought release from persecution and from the strong limits on their freedom of expression and religious practices in places like Soviet Russia, Eastern Europe, Korea, Vietnam, and Cuba.

This version of the better life narrative also appears to have a long pedigree in U.S. history, all the way back to the Puritans of New England seeking the freedom to practice their dissenter Protestant faith in the New World. We might add Irish Catholics escaping English restrictions on their politics and religion; Germans looking to avoid the political and religious restrictions of Bismark's *Kulturkampf*; and Eastern European Jews fleeing the murderous pogroms of the Russian Empire. Yet, as noted in the immigration history above, most of these groups were not received into the United States *because* of their persecuted status. The oppression they hoped to escape was almost beside the point, as far as the U.S. government was concerned. Nor did nineteenth-century Catholics and early twentieth-century Jews, for example, find a new home devoid of religious persecution. In the mid-nineteenth century, mobs burned Catholic churches and an entire political party with national reach, the American (or Know Nothing) party, grew out of anti-Catholic prejudice. Immigration restriction in the 1920s was designed explicitly to deter southern and eastern European Catholics and Jews. As a result, many Jews who did seek refuge from Hitler's march across Europe in the 1930s and 1940s were turned away from the United States on account of that restriction.

In reality, a purposeful immigration policy meant to offer a haven to refugees was, like the economic boom that greatly enlarged the American middle class, a product of the Second World War. In its aftermath, millions of refugees wandered the ruins of Europe, and President Harry Truman pushed to see the Displaced Persons Act passed to admit more of these refugees. Before much time had elapsed, as the Cold War emerged, U.S. refuge policies, such as the Refugee Relief Program of the 1950s and the Cuban refugee programs of the 1960s, openly favored those who labored under communist regimes. Even so, South Vietnamese refugees in the late 1970s found a safe harbor in the United States only because of advocacy by the Carter administration. Only in 1980 did the United States approve a comprehensive law aimed at outlining and systematizing the procedures for accepting refugees facing persecution, almost thirty years after the 1951 United Nations Convention Relating to the Status of Refugees and two decades after the United States had begun to more intentionally accept small numbers of refugees. Still, U.S. policies were often much stricter than those of other nations.[20]

Despite this checkered history, it is true that millions of people who suffered under deep persecution around the world have found in the United States relief and safety for themselves and their children. A Cuban American colleague vividly remembers the arbitrary restrictions on religion and art in her Cuban youth, as well as the poverty and the time her relatives spent in jail. She is now an activist and theologian, and she encourages her children to be creative and outspoken. In my own classroom, I taught theology both to Vietnamese Americans and to international priests and sisters from Vietnam, sometimes in the same classroom. Their experiences could not be more different. The Vietnamese priests and nuns emphasize how quietly they proceed at home, their institutions vulnerable to government interference or appropriation, their leaders occasionally carted off to prison. They strive not to contest government policy, even when it conflicts with their religious beliefs. Vietnamese American students, usually either refugees or the children of refugees, speak openly about their faith and their political views, and their neighbors and family members fundraise for prominent public shrines and run for office.

These stories capture an important truth about political and religious refuge in the United States, namely, that it does provide a better life for many. At the same time, in the past or the present, this better life was not offered to all those suffering persecution. Since U.S. military involvement in Afghanistan and Iraq began in the early 2000s, the government has frequently restricted the number of political refugees permitted to come to the United States from those two countries, even occasionally indefinitely delaying the entry of those whose persecution resulted in part from their assistance to U.S. forces. In late 2018 and early 2019, a caravan of Central Americans fleeing gang persecution back home waited in vain at a hastily constructed refugee camp in Tijuana, just south of the U.S. border. Most ended up turning back or accepting asylum in Mexico. Meanwhile, some U.S. government spokespersons, including the president, portrayed the caravan as a threat, even though many of the violent gangs they were fleeing had their origins in U.S. cities, not in Central America. Perhaps a little disingenuously, Americans still think of their country as a refuge for the persecuted seeking a better life. Buoyed by the stories of famous refugees—the physicists Albert Einstein and Enrico Fermi, writers like Elie Wiesel and Alexandr Solzhenitsyn, dancer Mikhail Baryshnikov, singer Gloria Estefan, and Google co-founder Sergei Brin—U.S. citizens hold to the *identity* of serving as a haven for those escaping political and religious persecution for better life, even if the truth is somewhat more complicated. That identity reinforces the humanitarian *ethics* implied, even if it sometimes functions more as an ideal than a reality.

IMMIGRANT THREAT

In 2015, Donald J. Trump opened his campaign for president with a speech that concerned itself with immigration. Speaking about immigrants from Mexico, he said,

> When Mexico sends its people, they're not sending their best. They're not sending you....They're sending people that have lots of problems, and they're bringing those problems with us. They're bringing drugs. They're bringing crime. They're rapists.[21]

The narratives we have examined thus far emphasize the United States as a haven for those seeking a better life, but another major cultural narrative imagines immigrants—today particularly immigrants from Latin America—as dangerous threats against which American families need protection. This narrative describes the United States as a "dumping ground" rather than a haven.[22] It emphasizes the violent criminal acts of a small number of unauthorized immigrants, even though such immigrants are statistically much less likely than U.S.-born citizens to commit crimes.[23] Immigrants in general, especially undocumented immigrants or immigrants from Mexico, come across as a faceless malevolent presence. Here is President Trump in 2018:

> We have people coming into the country, or trying to come in—and we're stopping a lot of them—but we're taking people out of the country. You wouldn't believe how bad these people are. These aren't people. These are animals.[24]

Even in milder evocations of the immigrant threat, focusing on the stealing of American jobs or the disproportionate use of government benefits, there is generally a call for protective measures, for a more substantial border wall, military-style tactics at the border, or mass deportations of unauthorized immigrants. After all, a threat—real or imagined—demands measures of protection.

Given the intense presence of this narrative among far-right groups and its association with a Republican president, more liberal Americans may feel that such a narrative resides at a comfortable distance from them. It is a right-wing story. But research suggests that it is not, at least not exclusively. The political scientists Emily M. Farris and Heather Silber Mohamed did a comprehensive study of photographs in three major mainstream newsmagazines—*Time*, *Newsweek*, and *US News and World Report*—from 2000 to 2010, and they found that coverage of immigration disproportionately emphasized unauthorized immigration at 54 percent, though only a quarter of immigrants are undocumented; and border enforcement at 40 percent, even though less than half of unauthorized immigrants cross the border—most overstay visas. They also cite a variety of studies of mainstream media texts that highlight negative portrayals of immigrants as threats and criminals. They note that press coverage of immigration rarely focuses on the millions of Latinx immigrants with legal papers.[25] In short, the portrayal of immigrants in threatening terms appears not only among conservatives or in conservative media but across the allegedly left-leaning mainstream media as well.

Nor is it new. In countless newspaper cartoons from the nineteenth century, for example, Irish immigrants are portrayed as brutish, often drunk, and involved in criminal activity. In 1856, the journalist and anti-Catholic politician Thomas Whitney wrote about the "invasion" of Catholic, mostly Irish, immigrants in the cities of the Eastern Seaboard and its impact on good Protestant Americans:

> Many a family that had lived comfortably on the proceeds of the honest industry of the husband and father was driven to want, and often forced to seek subsistence in other cities. Taxation was swelled in furnishing a support to the thousands of indigent and diseased paupers....Crime of every degree was increased five-fold, and the prisons were peopled with exotic felons. The spirit of drunkenness lurked in low haunts and fetid groggeries, or reeled obscenely through the public thoroughfares; and the loose brawl and the midnight scream usurped the places of order, decency, and sobriety.[26]

By the early twentieth century, even as Emma Lazarus's poem welcoming those seeking a better life was affixed to the Statue of Liberty, a new threat narrative associated especially Italian immigrants with all things evil and threatening. Immigrants from southern Italy were branded as political radicals and violent criminals, stealing American jobs and prone to "primitive" Catholic religious customs. Yet data from that time suggests that Italians were no more involved in radicalism or crime than any other group of the era.[27]

In the contemporary United States, the immigrant threat narrative has targeted Muslim immigrants on account of a perceived connection to terrorism, which does not hold up to scrutiny. Since September 11, 2001, the sociologist Charles Kurzman has been researching the involvement of U.S. Muslims in violent extremism, and he found such participation consistently a tiny phenomenon—in most years less than a few dozen people among millions of Muslims living in the United States. In 2018, it was fourteen people, and no incidents or arrests involved Muslim immigrants entering the United States illegally. No immigrants from countries restricted from entry (the so-called "Muslim ban") caused any deaths within the United States.[28] In fact, nearly all the violence inflicted by terrorists within the United States in 2018 was perpetrated by homegrown terror groups, most of them espousing white supremacy.[29] Kurzman points out that even in years closer to 9/11, "Levels of violent extremism were low because Muslim-American communities engaged in extensive self-policing, consistently denounced violence, sought policy change through political engagement, and were building community institutions to support healthy civic engagement."[30]

Despite the outsized role of immigrants from Muslim countries in threat narratives, the most common version of the threat narrative targets people of Latin American descent. The cultural anthropologist Leo Chavez speaks of a "Latino Threat Narrative," a cultural narrative that asserts the following:

> Latinos are not like previous immigrant groups, who ultimately became part of the nation. According to the assumptions and taken-for-granted "truths" inherent in this narrative, Latinos are unwilling or incapable of integrating, of becoming part of the national community. Rather, they are part of an invading force from south of the border that is bent on reconquering land that was formerly theirs (the U.S. Southwest) and destroying the American way of life.[31]

The Latino Threat Narrative appears in news reports and commentary, political cartoons, talk shows, popular nonfiction books, blogs, political speeches and debates, and even scholarly books. Chavez pays particular attention to "spectacles," media-saturated public events like the border surveillance of the Minutemen during the early 2000s, or bizarre controversies over the availability of organ transplants for undocumented Latinx children.

The "plot lines" of the Latino Threat Narrative include several familiar strands. Rhetoric portrays Latinx immigrants as criminals; Mexican immigration is renamed an "invasion"; accusations are made about Mexicans' refusal to learn English and divided loyalties; there are vague intimations of national security problems; and tales are told of excessive childbearing. These plot strands highlight perceived dangers in the reality of contemporary immigration from Mexico and other parts of Latin America, but these dangers are almost entirely imaginary or greatly exaggerated. In fact, a recent comprehensive study of crime and immigration data over four decades in forty municipalities demonstrates that there is a correlation between increasing immigration, much of it from Latin America, and *less* crime.[32] Three different U.S. government commissions across the twentieth century consistently found that immigrants commit crimes at a lower rate than the native born.[33]

We have already seen in the previous chapter how contemporary immigrants speak more English than European immigrants did at the turn of the twentieth century. Sociologists Richard Alba and Victor Nee have found that, compared to Asian immigrant families, more children and even some grandchildren of Mexican and other Latin American immigrants continue to speak Spanish at home, but this has not impaired their fluency in English, and a good number speak English exclusively at home, especially in the third generation.[34] Evidence today also suggests that bilingualism leads to better academic outcomes over time.[35] Mexican immigrants are also not as isolated or resistant to the mainstream as the Latino Threat Narrative alleges. Even in the first year of residence in the United States, 11 percent of migrants to rural areas and 17 percent of migrants to urban areas report friendships with Anglos, and after a decade and a half in the country, most of the friends of rural Mexican migrants are actually Anglos.[36]

Chavez devotes an entire chapter to the disturbing rhetoric around Mexican immigrant fertility in his book *The Latino Threat*. This part of the cultural narrative of threat highlights higher birthrates among Latinas, which substantially slowed in the last decade,[37] but it traffics in sexual stereotypes about the "hot Latina" as well as old Protestant American associations between Catholic ethnicities and a troubling overabundance of children.[38] It identifies a problem with "anchor babies," that is, with undocumented immigrants coming to the United States to give birth in order to obtain family reunification visas for parents. The logic of this trope, of course, is effectively undermined by the uncertain nature of the decades-long process that follows.[39] Underneath all these plot lines around fertility, however, lie racialized fears around demographic change, the idea that Latinx people are in some way "taking over," leaving whites behind. Chavez even points to a 1980s discourse about a *Reconquista* of the Southwest, featuring a cartoon of President George W. Bush sporting a T-shirt printed with "Viva Reconquista" standing next to Mexican President Vicente Fox, who wears a matching T-shirt featuring the words, "I love gullible gringo politicians."[40]

Such conclusions rely on conceiving of Mexican immigrants as permanently *other* and non-American. This not only bypasses actual data on immigrant incorporation over time but also makes American identity into an ethnic or racial category rather than a cultural or political one. This threat narrative also echoes earlier immigrant threat narratives, "a grand tradition of alarmist discourse about immigrants and their perceived negative impacts on society," and, like this one, legitimizes anti-immigrant public policies.[41] Before the Latin American "invasion," the threat was from disorderly Irishmen, Germans unwilling to learn English or assimilate, criminal Italians, and Chinese workers stealing jobs. Indeed, through a longer historical lens, the immigrant threat narrative fits uncomfortably well not just with age-old human tendencies toward xenophobia, but also with the white supremacist tradition in American storytelling, where the ethnically or racially *other* was portrayed as a violent and dangerous villain. It famously appears in the Puritan story that African Americans are children of Noah's cursed son Ham, but perhaps more memorably in those Westerns where American Indians prove brutal and mysterious raiders, or in more recent narco-thrillers (*Sicario*, Netflix's *Narcos*), where a virtuous white government agent faces off against a ruthless Latin American cartel man.

As such, while the threat narrative does not accurately reflect the reality of immigration, including immigration from Latin America, it does insidiously reinforce white nationalist notions of American identity. The American studies scholar Lee Bebout points out how in narratives like this "whiteness is constructed against a Mexican Other."[42] According to the threat narrative, those of us of European descent may also be the progeny of immigrants, but our ancestors were the "right" kind of immigrants, those from civilized (read: white) nations. "We" are fundamentally different from "them." The ethics implied in such distinctions are even more troubling. The United States must then be protected from "them," necessitating a more militaristic approach to border security and the greater use of deadly force at the border. Immigrants, especially Muslim and Mexican immigrants, become a kind of dangerous fifth column living among us. This makes space for public policies that, as we will see in coming chapters, Christian faith finds morally objectionable. This includes dividing families through deportation, both at the border itself and through raids inside the country. It also leads to the deportation of children or young adults who do not possess citizenship but who have no memory of living anywhere but the United States, the so-called Dreamers. It can even lead to a call for the rapid deportation of all ten million unauthorized immigrants at once, people with families, homes, and lives in this country.

ILLEGAL AND IMMORAL

At dinner one night at a Euro-American couple's house, the husband told me he disagreed with his in-laws' desire to deport all the illegal Mexicans, since they are Christian brothers and sisters; still, he could see how people thought it was morally wrong—it is wrong, he said. "That's why they call it illegal." At a parish school festival filled with members of both communities [Anglo and Mexican], a middle-aged father said matter-of-factly that immigration was fine as long as people were legal and the town was not "overrun."...A parishioner who was a sheriff's deputy did not worry that members of his department acting as immigration agents would disrupt the Mexican community's trust (as has been argued by many urban police chiefs). After all, they had violated the law.[43]

The third cultural narrative with considerable influence over the attitudes of receiving communities invokes the rule of law as a moral arbiter, separating "good" immigrants from "bad" immigrants. In the excerpt above, we see how the white parishioners in a Catholic parish equate "being illegal," that is, a lack of authorization to live in the United States, with being immoral. They observe, accurately, that a lack of legal status implies some kind of violation of immigration laws. But they also presume that such a violation has significant moral weight, that to be "illegal" is morally wrong in a serious way.

It is not necessarily obvious why this should be so. Many violations of the law do not elicit this kind of moral disdain. Illegal does not mean immoral in all matters. Speeding, underage drinking, rolling through a stop sign, using marijuana, and illegally downloading music, for example, are seldom considered to have much moral weight. For most Americans, texting behind the wheel or even driving under the influence of drugs or alcohol do not make one a bad person, even though they are both persuasively linked to countless traffic fatalities. Why has having or not having legal papers become a sign of whether one is a good or a bad person?

Some political rhetoric argues that what makes illegal immigration immoral is an association between a lack of legal status and persistent criminal behavior—murder, rape, drug smuggling, or even terrorism. While not a few people hold strongly to this presupposition, it does not stand up well to scrutiny. As already noted, there is no evidence connecting undocumented immigrants to terrorism. For instance, all the 9/11 hijackers had proper visas. And while there is actually very little research on unauthorized immigrants and crime, the research that exists points out that the incarceration rates of the undocumented are about half those of the native born.[44] This makes intuitive sense, since most unauthorized immigrants try to make themselves as invisible as possible to the authorities; they understand that even minor criminal activity can lead to deportation. The undocumented people I have known consistently drive the speed limit.

The division of immigrants into legal-good and illegal-bad, however, goes far beyond perceived connections with other criminal behavior. It essentially serves to combine the two cultural narratives already discussed, associating the undocumented with the threat narrative and immigrants who have legal papers with the better life narrative. When receiving community members who insist on this legal divide describe an "illegal immigrant," they generally speak in terms reminiscent of Chavez's Latino Threat Narrative. "Illegals" are presumed to be Mexican, criminal, unwilling to speak English, ready to take advantage of government services. When President Trump opened his campaign by speaking of Mexican immigrants as criminals, many supporters assumed he was referring only to Mexicans without papers, though he himself did not make such a distinction in the speech. Despite these associations, the reality of the undocumented looks quite different. Indeed, only half of unauthorized immigrants are Mexican, a figure that is dropping year by year, and more than half a million undocumented immigrants are from Europe or Canada.[45] During a year of research in a small Midwestern city, I was consistently struck by the distance between the image of "illegals" reflected in the rhetoric of local media and some residents and the actual lives of the many undocumented immigrants I knew. While I was talking to people with relatively stable lives, houses, and children, who volunteered at church, were learning to speak English, and were deeply committed to their faith, I heard others complain about criminals and "scofflaws" who took advantage of the system. This is not to say that I have never encountered an unauthorized immigrant taking advantage of the system, but it is far less common than many people suppose.

This narrative of morally dividing immigrants by legal status has a certain unassailable, taken-for-granted quality in American life, making it difficult to question. According to the Enlightenment political theory that gave birth to the U.S. republic, government is a social contract between the individuals in a society and those who rule them, because without such a contract people would engage in whatever selfish behavior they might like, resulting in chaos. Law is the embodiment of this contract, and it functions as a bulwark against the chaos. Accordingly, Americans associate violation of immigration law with chaos and instability, even though the lives of many unauthorized immigrants are quite stable. According to the Pew Research Center, 66 percent of unauthorized immigrants have been in the country for more than a decade, typically about fifteen years. More than 80 percent of Mexicans without papers have lived in the U.S. over a decade, typically about seventeen years. This is in part the result of increased immigration enforcement since the 1990s; people no longer come and go but stay and settle down. Thus, in reality, increased enforcement actually led to *more* unauthorized immigrants staying in the country.

Accordingly, unauthorized immigrants are no longer overwhelmingly men, but nearly half are women or children.[46] The undocumented are much more likely to live in two-parent households than the native born. Thus, by many measures their lives are more stable and less disorderly than those of native-born citizens.

The bigger problem may be an almost exclusive association between illegal immigration and Mexicans. In other words, for some people at least, it is not that Mexican immigrants are designated bad people when they come without legal permission, but rather that "illegals" are bad people because they are Mexicans, particularly poor Mexicans. Indeed, as noted in the previous chapter, throughout U.S. history negative stereotypes have been attached to particular racial, ethnic, or religious groups:

> Through much of the [nineteenth] century, Irish Catholic immigrants were seen as drunken barbarians living in urban squalor, and Chinese immigrants were perceived as inscrutable aliens unworthy of trust or citizenship. Mormons were crazed pagan extremists. Southern and Eastern European Catholics and Jews were people of inferior intelligence whose entry had to be restricted lest American civilization be "diluted."[47]

In his comprehensive analysis of Mexican and Mexican American stereotypes historically through the present, Lee Bebout points to recurring images of Mexican men as violent, primitive, lawless, and lazy, and Mexican women as exotic, sexy, and aggressively fertile.[48] Many of my own students have witnessed what I have catalogued in my own research, that the members of receiving communities complain that Mexican immigrants are messy, noisy, undisciplined with their children, unwilling to follow rules.[49] All these pejorative images make it a simple matter for many Americans to react with, at best, annoyance toward "illegal Mexicans" and, at worst, anxiety and fear. Such reactions do not always emerge as something conscious or explicit. Indeed, the political scientist Efrén O. Pérez recently demonstrated an implicit bias among whites against Latinx immigrants in comparison with white immigrants.[50] Ethnic stereotypes about Mexicans and other Latin Americans by association clearly play some role in the case against illegal immigration as inherently immoral.

Again, this is not to deny that persons in the United States without legal papers have violated the law. But the U.S. legal system views illegal acts, including immigration violations, on a spectrum. For the last seven years, the majority of unauthorized immigrants have entered the country by legally obtaining a visa to visit the United States and then overstaying it.[51] Overstaying a visa is a civil rather than a criminal violation. Crossing the border illegally for the first time is a misdemeanor criminal act, in addition to being a civil violation, or the legal equivalent of trespassing, minor possession of alcohol, or initial possession of marijuana in some states. Indeed, when many deportees are described as "criminals," this is often the crime they stand accused of. Deportation or other crimes followed by further attempts at crossing can substantially increase the seriousness of the offense. Unlawful presence itself is not necessarily a crime, though it generally has severe repercussions on one's ability to secure a legal visa. Faced with this nuanced, complex system, only summarily described here, a simple distinction between good legal immigrants and bad illegal ones does not seem as tenable. In considering this cultural narrative, it is also important to remember that technically speaking, persons cannot be "illegal," only the acts they perform. Accordingly, we generally do not speak, for example, of those who speed on the highway as "illegal drivers."

Dividing immigrants into categories based on legal status has a comforting aspect to it for many people in receiving communities. It appears to clearly communicate the difference between friend and foe. The moral truth, however, is considerably more complicated. Citizens and immigrants with permanent visas may also find that the legal-moral distinction allows them to affirm the virtue of their own position. Scholars like Brebout and Chávez point out that stereotypes affixed to "illegals," usually illegal Mexicans, imply a contrasting image of American citizens as industrious, orderly, modern, and law abiding, with a reasonable number of children. Others use this cultural narrative about dangerous illegals to celebrate the proper arrival of their ancestors to the United States, even though the current distinction between lawful and unlawful entry is a product of the immigration laws of the 1920s. Finally, the legal-moral distinction makes for a clear and exacting code of ethics. Legal immigrants stay; illegal immigrants go home. It saves receiving communities the trouble of understanding what motivated people to migrate, or of empathizing with what they have suffered, or even of seeing them as persons. It does not necessitate self-examination about our role in migration systems or introduce messy conversations about mercy. It is simple and clear, even if it makes us less humane in the process.

BEYOND THE BIG THREE NARRATIVES

I selected the three narratives examined above—the better life narrative, the threat narrative, and the rule of law narrative—because of their omnipresence in the discourse of U.S. receiving communities. But they do not exhaust the stories told about why people migrate and how migration works. Other common narratives include, for example, the notion that immigrants do the work native-born Americans disdain, jobs the theologian Gemma Tulud Cruz calls "3D" (dirty, dangerous, and demeaning) or SALEP (shunned by all laborers except the poor).[52] This story appears to appreciate immigrant contributions, but it also draws attention away from illicit or even dangerous working conditions, and it carefully hides the long history of employers recruiting a lower-paid class of workers on purpose to maximize their revenues. Another more obscure narrative positions immigrants as wisdom figures, photo negatives of American superficiality, materialism, or spiritual bankruptcy. In a kind of turnabout of the better life narrative, their comments, teaching, or virtuous lifestyle awaken afflicted or jaded Americans to a better life (think of Mr. Miyagi in the 1984 film *Karate Kid*). Again, this narrative seems to admire what immigrants bring to the nation, but it also exoticizes them, turning them into caricatures instead of people.

By including these less influential narratives from receiving communities, we are still examining only one side of the story. The ethicist Tisha Rajendra argues that we should be wary of such one-sidedness in cultural narratives:

> Dominant narratives often obscure the experiences and insights of those on the margins of society, including migrants....We must pay special attention to the narratives that represent the voices and experiences of those who have traditionally been ignored or marginalized, as well as to the narratives of the "victims of history"—those who are no longer here to tell their tale. This is not because these

overlooked or forgotten narratives are automatically more faithful to reality; they may or may not be. But those narratives can challenge the *mainstream* narrative and enable us to look for what Margaret Urban Walker calls "inconsistencies, lies, and embarrassments." The narratives of marginalized voices can also help expose those places where the dominant narrative merely reproduces the interests of the powerful. Therefore, incorporating the perspectives of the powerless and forgotten helps narratives become more faithful to reality.[53]

Accordingly, we turn now to cultural narratives often less well known in receiving communities, that is, the cultural narratives that motivate migrants themselves and help them make sense of their experience. The next chapter will attempt to tell those stories, with some additional attention as well to the cultural narratives of those left behind by migrants, the neighbors and family members back in sending countries who have their own tales to tell.

Chapter Four

LONGING AND LOSS

Migration According to Migrants and Sending Communities

One summer I taught a graduate course on faith and culture, and I included a short section on immigration. To begin, I invited the class to share their families' migration stories, at least insofar as they knew the stories and felt comfortable. Some of the students knew almost nothing, their families having been in the United States for generations, and the stories lost to history, a textbook case of immigrant amnesia. Others shared what they knew of family journeys from some decades ago. But not a small number of the students were immigrants themselves (this was in Southern California), and several seemed to have been waiting for someone to ask. We heard dramatic and sometimes deeply painful accounts of dangers and hardships, fear and trauma, and gratitude for finding their way to a new life. By the end of several of these stories, students born in the United States were flabbergasted at what their classmates had endured.

Just as these personal accounts of family migration look very different between migrants and longtime residents, so too do larger cultural narratives appear quite different. The cultural narratives of migrants serve a fundamentally different purpose than those told in receiving communities. Both kinds of narratives look to make sense of the motives that drive migrants and the consequences of their journeys, but with different trajectories. Receiving communities construct migration narratives with an eye toward their own identity as a destination community in the present and the past. As noted in the previous chapter, such narratives often invoke imaginative reconstructions of ancestors' migration stories, stories shaped by amnesia and nostalgia. These cultural narratives are less concerned with accurately reporting on how migration works than they are with asserting the identity of a local community—usually as open or properly resistant to newcomers—and with expressing a practical ethics that demarcates who should be welcomed and who should be sent packing.

Migrant communities themselves, however, form and retell cultural narratives about migration with the purpose of justifying and finding meaning in their own experiences, but also offering practical advice to other migrants. Some also wish to be able to explain what they have seen and done to the communities from which they departed. Because these families and communities are made up of actual migrants who are making or have made their journey within living memory, there is much less immigrant amnesia, except some produced by traumatized parents who play down the dangers or suffering involved when speaking to their children. There may, however, be significant nostalgia. Longing for what was left behind may produce a rosier view of the sending community, or, in contrast, the depth of loss may lead to an exaggeration of the differences between present success and previous hardships. Even so, there is less opportunity and motive to completely edit out the ambiguous or difficult elements of the journey of migration; migrant cultural narratives contain on average less idealizing and more practical details. Indeed, most migrants remain aware that cultural narratives have a shadow side, a more cynical or tragic version of the story.

In this chapter, we explore three major cultural narratives of migrants, often interrelated, most exhibiting a shadow side. The first narrative appears to echo the receiving communities' narrative of the better life, a variation of the American Dream. Like the better life narrative, it largely focuses on the economic prospects of migrants. It has, however, a more provisional and less ideological quality to it. The migrants' better life narrative does not necessarily assume that American society is built for social mobility or presents endless opportunities. The narrative sees North American receiving communities as providing concrete and often specific opportunities to address the economic challenges that families face back home. For a great many, these concrete opportunities are seen as a temporary pathway, with the ultimate purpose of returning home. For others, the relocation was always meant to be permanent, usually because circumstances in the homeland will never accommodate one's personal or family ambitions, at least not for the foreseeable future.

A related and often consequent cultural narrative has to do with migration for the sake of family, usually to reunite separated families. Even temporary migration can prove to be more long term than expected or even permanent, and this applies pressure either for the breakup of families or their reunification through additional migration. Because family ties are often quite strong, and the loss of them sharply felt, this narrative can prove powerful enough to inspire behavior others find baffling or unexpectedly risky, such as relocating young children in the middle of a school year, migrating while pregnant, or even hiring a smuggler for a teenage son or daughter traveling without a parent. Finally, also compelling for migrants is the cultural narrative of escape. According to this narrative, the situation at home can no longer be described as a challenge or a problem. It has become an unbearable crisis or an imminent threat. This is the narrative, for example, of political or religious refugees.

These three, of course, are not the only cultural narratives associated with migrant communities, but they are the most influential and widespread. At the end of this chapter we will take a brief look at some of the major cultural narratives of sending communities. As in the case of receiving communities, sending communities have other identity-related reasons for forming and retelling cultural narratives of migration. They must make sense of who they are as a community whose sons and daughters feel they must leave. In doing so, they may embrace the reasons migrants present or they may reject them. Loss, envy, or resentment may play a strong role in these narratives. People may even forget why their family members or neighbors left in the first place, exhibiting a certain amnesia, and nostalgia may precipitate a certain romanticism either about their own communities and subsequent vitriol against the receiving communities or flattering views of the receiving communities that unnecessarily darken their views of their own homelands. But before discussing the specifics of these sending community narratives, we turn to a more thorough description of migrant community narratives.

A BETTER DEAL

In a short excerpt from the section title page above, the Ecuadorian American writer Karla Cornejo Villavicencio reports how her parents migrated to the United States in order to earn enough to pay off debts to their disagreeable extended family.[1] Families in the rural Guatemalan town of Todos Santos—All Saints—send young people to the United States in search of the kind of social safety net the Guatemalan government does not provide, including to get an education beyond elementary school and to provide seed money to build a house.[2] An Indian doctor I knew in New York had as his deepest ambition the desire to teach prospective doctors in medical school, but he lacked the connections and social standing to attain such a position back home. In Isabel Wilkerson's magisterial account of the Great Migration, another doctor, Robert Joseph Pershing Foster, opts to leave Monroe, Louisiana, for California in 1953 because he was barred as an African American man from working in the local hospital and because "Pershing did not want to be paid with buttermilk or the side of a freshly killed hog and did not want to deliver babies in somebody's kitchen."[3] In all these cases, people were searching for something specific that they could not achieve or find back home. The first two imagined migration as a temporary solution to financial dilemmas. The doctors, however, understood their decision as permanent, since there was little chance of finding the professional success they sought in their native places. But all three came with particular, commonsense goals, characteristic of the cultural narrative of migrant communities. In contrast to the more amorphous economic dream of a "better life" that makes the rounds in receiving communities, we might refer to this more specific, practical dream as a better deal narrative.

As we learned in chapter 2, the better deal is often for the family or household rather than for the individual. Even Dr. Pershing Foster intended to bring his family to a world where they did not have to bow before white people. The classic story of Mexican migration to the United States begins not with unemployment but with underemployment. Money earned proves insufficient to provide for specific needs of the household—to pay for children's educational costs, to build a house, to pay for medical care. This leads to a collective decision to send someone to the United States to work and then send money home as remittances. An international student from Vietnam told me how her sister came to the United States through a similar family decision-making process. Some of today's migrants from Central America make such decisions when extortion from gangs takes so much of the proceeds from a family business that the business can no longer fully provide for the family. I have heard various migrants talk about how a more encouraging business climate in receiving communities allows them to build up a business they could not back at home.

While the lion's share of migrants may focus on the needs of their family, there will always be those who migrate out of personal ambition unrelated to their family's economic situation. They too seek a better deal than they can see for themselves at home, but their sense of what that might be is less specific and practical. Recall the young man in the first chapter who all his life thought about going to the United States to seek his fortune. Indeed, their journeys more closely resemble the better life narrative that circulates among U.S. receiving communities, where a lone protagonist follows a somewhat nebulous dream for the future. Most will likely stay, but even those who do not may look on their time as a migrant nostalgically as a youthful adventure. Yet, even when the better deal has more to do with an individual's ambition, such as with my doctor friend, the migrant often seeks his or her family's permission to go, and there is expectation of sending money home should they find success.

These takes on the better deal narrative demonstrate how specific institutional factors in the local economy and power structure shape the development of this narrative. Todos Santos could not get any support from a government they saw as corrupt. In a recent visit to a migrant shelter, I met countless men from Central America who talked about how government and law enforcement did nothing to help anyone. In the 1990s and 2000s, many Mexicans from smaller farms could no longer compete in the post-NAFTA economic integration, and migrating to the United States, usually without papers, formed one storied path to a better economic situation. African American professionals in the Jim Crow South had no access to white-led institutions, which were more ubiquitous and better funded. Even today's professional migrants speak of institutional obstacles to their success, including closed social networks that control access to resources or jobs, as in the case of my doctor friend, or frustratingly onerous or narrow institutional pathways to success. A former professor of mine found the burdensome requirements of German academia too much for her and unconducive to her pursuit of edgier research topics. At the same time, these economic obstacles may actually lead to the creation and growth of institutions that facilitate migration, as with the considerable medical training apparatus in the Philippines that prepares doctors, nurses, and other medical professionals to work abroad.

Because the better deal narrative usually remains practical and specific, it resists the kind of broad evaluation afforded the better life narrative. Enough people succeed in their particular ambitions that the narrative continues to appear plausible. I myself have met more than one former migrant who returned home after having earned enough to build a house or start a successful business. The town of Todos Santos is no longer deeply impoverished and is dotted with American-style homes, thanks to family members in the United States. My doctor friend did end up teaching at a medical school, and Dr. Pershing Foster found access to white-led institutions in California, though he did not avoid discrimination entirely.

But clearly many people do not achieve what they hoped for themselves and their families. One deportee interviewed as part of the Migrant Border Crossing Study, identified as Miguel, had been living in Arizona supporting his wife, children, and recently widowed mother when a trip to use a pay phone led to his being questioned by the police and then deported. He gave up after that, complaining of racial profiling by the police and a lack of work during an economic recession. Another interviewee, Diego, talked about life in Phoenix as a disappointing grind: "One goes from home to work, and back home again. It's like living in a prison."[4] In the same study, a majority of deportees reported they would *not* try to cross again in the near future.[5] Even highly educated, professional immigrants with legal status can find their hopes crushed. Living in New York many years ago, I met at least one former college professor working as a taxi driver. Countless professional women endure employer sexual harassment they feel they cannot report lest they lose their green card sponsorship.

Receiving communities may not ever see any direct evidence as to whether or not their cultural narratives pan out as they expect, but migrants and their families will. In those cases where the better deal never materializes, they must come to terms with the disappointment. Thus, migrant community cultural narratives often come accompanied by "shadow versions," where the hope is turned upside down and some form of explanation is offered. One such version I have heard in the context of my own research is a kind of shadow narrative of hypocrisy. According to this narrative, the receiving country promises what it never had any intention of delivering. For example, many undocumented immigrants speak of the hypocrisy embedded in openly recruiting unauthorized immigrants for particular jobs or to certain industries that they dominate such as construction or hospitality, while at the same time there exists no pathway to legal status. They are hired, often with winks and nods about their lack of status, but their employment leads either to exploitation they cannot protest, such as unsafe conditions and illegal wages, or to psychological insecurity born of permanent uncertainty about their future. Even authorized, professional migrants encounter this narrative of hypocrisy. "In Ontario [Canada] in 1996, every medical school graduate was guaranteed an internship after passing the medical examinations, but only about 24 of the 500 foreign-trained doctors who had passed their required examinations in Canada were given internship positions."[6]

Another shadow narrative finds less fault with the host country and more simple poignant tragedy. The theologian Daniel Groody reports on a Mexican *corrido*, a tragic narrative ballad, about two teenage brothers crossing the Rio Grande hoping to change the economic situation of their family. One of them drowns in the river, and the remaining brother is traumatized by the experience. He finds he cannot bear to reveal the tragedy to his parents, increasing the burden for him.[7] Even when the consequences are less dire, immigrant communities describe their experiences in terms of tragedy, unexpected life-destroying circumstances. Young undocumented women and men have spoken to me of how unprepared they were for the stresses that emerged in the new country, including temptations to drugs and alcohol, depression, marital problems, and all-encompassing loneliness.[8] Groody speaks of the collective impact of endless hard labor, discrimination and scapegoating, and low wages and economic exploitation as a kind of immigrant way of the cross, a metaphor we explore more fully when we turn to theology in chapter 9.[9] For some, however, this background of temptation and tragedy provided a backdrop for a counternarrative, one where immigrants are not victims of circumstance but are led to a spiritual or religious conversion that redeems their suffering. Conversion sets them on a more stable path, one often characterized by religious commitment and greater focus on marriage and family.[10] This focus on family relationships echoes an entirely different cultural narrative about migration, what we might call the migration-for-family narrative.

FOR THE SAKE OF THE FAMILY

In my own research, I have encountered a common twist in the better deal narrative recounted above. Many nonprofessional migrants fully intend to return to their homeland once they have achieved the goals they set for themselves, such as building a house for one's family back home or stabilizing family finances. Some obviously do return; in sending countries like Mexico or the Philippines, it is not uncommon to meet former migrants who have returned for good. Yet others stay long enough to establish families or to send for spouses and children they initially planned would remain at home. Eventually the formation of families in the receiving country makes return less and less plausible, especially as children grow older, having lived their whole lives in the United States. Gradually the cultural narrative of migration shifts from focus on resolving an economic problem back home to supporting a family based in the United States. Parents tell their children, "We moved here for you."

While this may seem like the natural course of things, the focus on families living stateside is abetted by institutional factors. U.S. migration law since 1965 has favored family reunification, and fiancés/fiancées, spouses, and minor children are not subject to the kinds of quotas that delay migration almost indefinitely. Perhaps more unexpectedly, the increase in immigration enforcement and border fortification since the 1990s has made it much more expensive and difficult for persons to cross back and forth without papers. Uncertain of their ability to return to the United States, people stay. They may send for their families, and those families become settled and established. When families do become separated by deportation, parents become motivated to return. Indeed, the Migrant Border Crossing Study found that even if migrants had originally come to the United States for economic reasons, a majority of those who intended to return, soon did so in order to reunite with family in the United States.[11] All this seems to reflect the realities of contemporary border control. As a Border

Patrol agent reminded me recently, the present border enforcement regimen was built to detain and deter single men with a history of crossing back and forth to work, but the actual situation at the border today includes many women and children, families traveling together, and even "unaccompanied" minor children, alone or in the custody of siblings or other relatives who are not their parents. Some of that is motivated by family reunification, though some is also the outcome of developments in Central America, as we will see in the next section.

The migration-for-family narrative has different strands emphasized by different migration flows. For Mexicans and Central Americans it has a practical streak oriented to stability: "The 'Latino/a American Dream' is increasingly connected to keeping one's family together and fostering an emerging sense of 'place' and 'home' in the United States."[12] Korean communities emphasize how the hard work and suffering of the immigrant generation can be redeemed by the educational, professional, and financial success of the U.S.-born generation, though the restless ambition generated can become oppressive to both generations.[13] Filipino professionals in the United States see themselves as working multiple jobs both to support economically challenged extended families back home but also to sponsor and provide for recently migrated relatives. The migration-for-family narrative in that community is resolutely oriented to the larger extended family.[14]

As often happens with matters of family, however, cultural narratives of commitment and sacrifice can overtake a considerably more complicated reality. Migration puts tremendous stress on families. When families do not migrate together, the resulting separation can lead to divorce and family rifts or to the development of parallel families in each country, just as easily as it motivates family reunification. Children in U.S. schools are directed toward rapid English acquisition and socialization into the American educational system. Their parents often adapt at a much slower pace, especially if they are working multiple jobs to make a living or send money back home. The resulting "dissonant acculturation" leads to family tensions and the breakdown of parental authority, and in some situations makes children vulnerable to criminal subcultures.[15] Finally, deportation frequently separates parents from their children, sometimes even leading to the placement of children in the foster care system and adoption. Migrants are aware of these possibilities; the shadow side of the migration-for-family narrative is an implicit narrative of "families destroyed by migration."

MIGRATION AS FLIGHT

During visits to a migrant shelter in 2019 and 2020, I encountered many Central American men whose accounts were narratives of escape from gang violence. Indeed, most anyone who has spoken with Central Americans hoping for asylum in the United States lately can report stories of ever increasing extortion from gangs coupled with threats of violence toward those who fail to pay, tales of pressure on young men to join and threats to their lives if they refuse, and catastrophic violence toward family members who resist gang hegemony. These stories fit the pattern of a long-term cultural narrative we might call an escape or flight narrative, where a crisis in one's own community becomes so severe and threatening that departure and migration appear the only way out. It is a narrative that appears not only in the stories of Central Americans requesting asylum today, but also in the reports of all refugees, of LGBT persons experiencing discrimination or violence at home, and of women afflicted by domestic violence whose complaints have no force in their homelands.

Even if some of these stories are more recent, the escape narrative has a long pedigree. Irish immigrants fled the starvation of the potato famine in the 1840s. Jews fled Nazi oppression, though they were sometimes turned away. Escape is a principal narrative of the Great Migration, the movement of African Americans out of the Jim Crow South during the twentieth century. Southern Blacks were hemmed in by segregation laws that regulated nearly every aspect of their lives, relegating them to inferior schools, dirty waiting rooms, and back doors to restaurants and stores. They could not share a restroom, a staircase, a streetcar with whites. They had no recourse when employers mistreated them. Courts would not enforce any laws that protected them. And they were lynched with impunity: "In spectacles that went on for hours, black men and women were routinely tortured and mutilated, then hanged or burned alive, all before festive crowds of as many as several thousand white citizens, children in tow, hoisted on their fathers' shoulders to get a better view."[16] Once it became clear that African Americans in the South could flee to northern and western cities and find jobs there, they went.

The shadow side of the escape narrative past and present arises when migrants' flight from danger fails—when they do not escape.

Indeed, Anne Frank's is among those Jewish families who applied to migrate to the United States during the Second World War but were refused. Migrants hoping to escape may find agents and asylum officers skeptical of their claims, especially if the latter have been lied to before. A Border Patrol agent once confided to me that he assumed that most asylum claims by Central Americans were false. Sometimes this kind of skepticism has lethal consequences. A young woman named Yadira escaped to the United States after challenging the local gang that murdered her brother. Deported back, she was killed. Constantino Morales, a police officer from the Mexican state of Guerrero, fled to the United States after his investigation of a drug cartel brought threats to his life. After a routine traffic stop, he was deported and then shot to death a few months later.[17] Nor does arriving in the United States always amount to safe escape. On Long Island, some migrant teenagers who fled gang violence in El Salvador find themselves face-to-face with MS-13 gang members in their new high schools; a few even end up detained in immigration facilities along with gang members.[18] The resulting narrative arguing that "no place is safe" has some basis in reality.

MAKING SENSE OF AN EXODUS

In the beginning chapter, we looked at how migration inevitably involves three different communities—migrants, those who receive them in the new land, and those they left back home. We hear much more about the first two than the last. Researchers in receiving countries like the United States, Canada, or Germany understandably place less emphasis on the sending community as they attempt to come to terms with the ways their own countries have been changed by migration. The sending community experience does not lend itself to narrative the way migration might. There is less of a comprehensible plot here—people leave; life goes on. Migration works dramatic alterations in receiving communities. People arrive speaking different languages, behaving according to distinct cultural expectations. That change feels like a story. In a sending community, changes occur gradually and over time. People may fail to notice. Hundreds of thousands of Americans have migrated to Mexico, but very few people in the United States have noticed. Sending communities only begin to tell a story once a critical mass of people has left, or when a critical mass returns bearing gifts, innovations, and customs they acquired elsewhere. Family stories turn into larger cultural narratives about the exodus.

In the 1990s, I studied Spanish in the Dominican Republic in the midst of a huge migration wave of Dominican migrants moving to New York and New Jersey (the Dominican immigrant population in the United States quadrupled between 1980 and 2000).[19] I found that migration to the United States was on everyone's mind. I was even directed to a then-recent Dominican film, *Nueba Yol*, with Dominican comedian Luisito Martí playing one of his iconic characters, Balbuena, on an ill-fated voyage to New York in search of work. Much of the film chronicles the good-natured character's encounter with bureaucratic hassles, unfriendly New Yorkers, unemployment, and discrimination, all of which compel him to eventually go home. Partially an old-style tale of a rube in the big city, the film articulated at least one cultural narrative of sending communities—a narrative of resentment. This story portrays the United States as an unwelcoming, bigoted, material-istic land that corrupts earnest migrants. While I was studying Spanish in the capital, one of my teachers answered my query about what I should say to Dominicans in New York in a way that highlighted this narrative. He said that I should tell them that missing their children's lives was not worth a pair of expensive sneakers.

Naturally, other sending communities develop a more positive story to tell about migrants leaving home. In a manner that fits with the migrant better deal narrative, many Latin American sending com-munities see a jaunt to the United States to work as almost a rite of passage that brings resources back to the community. This is migra-tion as community assistance. In a small town in the state of Puebla, Mexico, I found that the town plaza had been redone with money from the United States. In San Cristóbal Totonicapán in Guatemala, a brother and sister started a business building American-style houses for families receiving money from the United States.[20] Fully 11 percent of Guatemala's gross domestic product in 2017 came from remittances, and sending households that receive this money experienced reduced poverty, better health outcomes because of increased access to basic utilities, and more childhood education.[21] A Guatemalan Catholic priest summed up this narrative regarding his own community, saying, "Our people go north and work day and night, to send money back to build homes, to buy land, to help their families. That is the life of Todos Santos."[22]

There are, of course, other cultural stories people in sending communities tell to make sense of the departure of their loved ones. A less talked about but strongly present cultural narrative in sending communities is a narrative of loss. Once on a trip to central Mexico, I visited the mother of a Mexican immigrant I knew. She wept often during my time there, lamenting her son's departure and worrying about him constantly. Even within countries internal migration can provoke a cultural narrative of loss. More than half a century after my father left Indiana to move to California, my cousin shared with my wife how much my siblings and I missed out on by growing up far away from the family. On the other hand, the migrant narrative of escape or flight has its equivalent in a kind of narrative of relief in sending communities. Cuban parents who sent their unaccompanied children to the United States during Operation Pedro Pan in 1965 and Vietnamese parents who sent their children out alone just before the fall of Saigon in the early 1970s suffered loss, but their main reaction was relief that their children would not have to grow up with hardship and repression.

This brief examination of sending community narratives brings this section on cultural narratives to a close, though we will continue to reference and evaluate these narratives going forward. Presenting these narratives has largely been a descriptive and evaluative task. Though many people in receiving, migrant, and sending communities view these cultural narratives as authoritative and prescriptive, I have argued that we should approach them more critically, evaluating to what extent they reflect the complex realities of migration, especially as we uncovered them in the chapter on the empirical reality of migration. As a Catholic theologian, however, I also believe that people of faith, or of no faith, should evaluate these narratives based on the traditions of meaning that have been handed to us and we see as normatively shaping our view of migration and other social issues. For Christians, this means looking to the Bible, to the sweep of Christian history, as well as to contemporary Christian ethics and theology. Among Christians, Catholics also look to the principles of Catholic social teaching. But before we move into those specific areas, we will step back and look at how faith traditions, in general, view migration and how they might see it differently.

Section Three

SACRED NARRATIVES AND MIGRATION

Now the Lord said to Abram, "Go from your country and your kindred and your father's house to the land that I will show you."

—Genesis 12:1

Now after they had left, an angel of the Lord appeared to Joseph in a dream and said, "Get up, take the child and his mother, and flee to Egypt, and remain there until I tell you; for Herod is about to search for the child, to destroy him." Then Joseph got up, took the child and his mother by night, and went to Egypt, and remained there until the death of Herod. This was to fulfill what had been spoken by the Lord through the prophet, "Out of Egypt I have called my son."

—Matthew 2:13–15

Ibrahim said [to his father], "Peace be on you; I will pray to my Lord for your forgiveness: Verily, He is affectionate towards me. And I will go away from you and from those whom you call upon besides Allah: And I will call on my Lord: Perhaps, by my prayer to my Lord, I shall be not condemned."

—Qur'an 19:47–48, sixth edition of Holmdel translation for young people

Chapter Five

MIGRATION AS HOLY HISTORY

Each of the cultural narratives we examined in the last two chapters had limitations, despite the fact that they often frame the way we think about migration in North America. They have lights and shadows, some of them more shadow than light. But these cultural narratives are not the only ways of framing migration in the world today. I noted at the very beginning of the book how common a phenomenon migration has been in human history, and the world's great religious traditions have often included migration in their stories and teachings, some more than others. These stories and teachings may help us make better sense of the reality of migration in all its complexity than the cultural narratives have done. As we will see in this chapter, the Abrahamic traditions in particular view migration sympathetically, in part because the major figures of their foundations—Abraham, Moses, Jesus, Muhammad—were all migrants of one sort or another. We may also find that other religious traditions, such as Buddhism, have something important to say about migration.

RELIGIOUS VIEWS OF TIME

Judaism, Christianity, and Islam are sometimes referred to as the Abrahamic religious traditions, after Abraham of Ur. Abraham (*Avraham* in Hebrew and *Ibrahim* in Arabic) was the ancient—some would say legendary—patriarch chosen by God in the Jewish and Christian Scriptures and in the Qur'an to be progenitor, literal or figurative, to all those who cling to the one God. In the Jewish and Christian Scriptures, God calls on Abraham to leave his native land and his family and to journey to a land he does not yet know (Gen 12:1). In the Qur'an, the focus is on Ibrahim's argument and eventual separation from his family and community over their refusal to abandon their many gods (see Qur'an 19:41–49). He does indeed migrate (Qur'an 29:26), but it is only after much effort spent trying to persuade his polytheistic family and hometown of the error of their ways. And just as all Abrahamic traditions share the story of this early migrant, they all three also share a generally positive view of migration itself.

In all three religious traditions, God reveals a divine message intervening in the history of a community. For Jews, God led the Israelites out of slavery in Egypt and made a covenant with them. Christians see Jesus as God's decisive intervention in world history, to bring about salvation. Muslims look to the Qur'an, revealed by the one God (*Allah* means "the God" in Arabic) to Muhammad through the angel Gabriel (Arabic *Jibreel*) to set human beings on the path to salvation. Christians call this notion of God intervening in human history *salvation history*, and that history is also posited to have a conclusion when salvation will come to the world in a final and complete way. In Judaism, the messiah or messianic age will come and "repair the world." In Christianity, Jesus promised to return and definitively establish his reign on earth, even as he promised resurrection to believers on a final Day of Judgment. Islam also promises a final resurrection on the Day of Judgement leading to life in God's presence or, for the damned, without God. All three religions posit this eschatological (final) future, though it is perhaps more central in Christianity and Islam.

For the Abrahamic traditions, this joint focus on God's involvement in particular events and a future fulfillment give time a linear shape. This linear shape to time turns individual lives, the history of communities of faith, and human history as a whole into a kind of migration story; life moves on from event to event until we find our true home with God at the end. As we will see, ancient Christians often described themselves as strangers or immigrants on the earth. This view of time contrasts dramatically with the cyclical nature of time in religious traditions with their roots in South Asia, such as Hinduism, Buddhism, and Jainism. In these faith traditions, humans, like all creatures, are trapped in *samsara*, the often-frustrating cycle of continual reincarnation or rebirth. The point of spiritual practice in these traditions is to escape that cycle, for example, by detachment from desire in Buddhism, or recognition of the soul's unity with God in Advaita Vedanta Hinduism. There is no communal or global eschatological finale as in the Abrahamic religions, and there is disagreement within these traditions as to what such escape actually looks like.

This cyclical notion of time, however, may make space for thinking about migration in a different way. If the point is to escape the cycle of rebirth, then one is, in a sense, looking to become a migrant, to leave one's home. Indeed, in Hindu tradition, after one completes the task of raising a family and contributing to society, one may become a holy wanderer, a *sannyasin*, in hope of finding one's way to *moksha*, that is, freedom from *samsara*. The religious studies scholar John Thompson argues that Buddhism may be understood as defining the path toward liberation from *samsara* as a kind of *spiritual* immigration. The Buddhist profession of faith has followers pledging to "take refuge" in the Buddha, the Dharma (the Buddhist way), and the Sangha (the Buddhist community), implying that one becomes a kind of refugee in search of enlightenment. In Theravada Buddhism this ideally means relocating to a monastery as part of the search. In Mahayana Buddhism the adherent seeks guidance from the *bodhisattva*, the person who has completed their spiritual immigration toward liberation from *samsara* but journeys back to help others. In the Pure Land tradition of Buddhism, trust in the Amitabha Buddha leads one to a temporary paradise on the way to liberation, a place where it is much easier to reach enlightenment.[1] Thus, while the Abrahamic linear sense of time naturally leads to one thinking of one's life or community as a kind of migration toward a final conclusion, even in the cyclical time of South Asian religions there is a possibility for making use of migration as a metaphor for the spiritual search.

FOUNDATIONAL FIGURES

The relationship between migration and the Abrahamic traditions, however, is more than just a matter of a congenial view of time. Migration figures prominently in the foundational stories of each of the Abrahamic religions, beyond just the story of Abraham himself.

In Judaism, the paradigmatic experience of migration is that of the exodus, the movement of the Israelites out of slavery in Egypt into the promised land. God delivers them through this act of migration led by Moses. As we will see in the next chapter, that experience shapes a more hospitable attitude toward foreigners in their own land. Exile is also a substantial part of Jewish history, the Babylonian exile in the sixth century before the Common Era and various other forcible and voluntary movements that constitute the Jews as a people in diaspora. The great rabbis and sages who populate and form the stories and judgments of the Talmud—the great commentary on the Torah, the initial books of the Bible—come both from diasporic lands like Babylonia and from the traditional Israelite homeland.

In Judaism, experiences of exodus, exile, and diaspora have shaped complex responses to the notion of assimilation in a foreign land. The long experience of anti-Jewish discrimination in medieval and early modern Europe bred caution among Jews about their relations with the dominant Christian culture. Post-Enlightenment movements toward the political emancipation of the Jews in Western Europe promised a more harmonious and secular society for those who did assimilate. In the United States and Canada, despite the continued presence of anti-Semitic attitudes and even hate crimes, that promise has largely been fulfilled. Jews live and work in nearly every strata of North American society. But in Europe, the German Nazi Final Solution nearly exterminated European Jews entirely. The *Shoah*, or Holocaust, linked Judaism more securely to Zionism, the movement to return to the biblical homeland as a refuge.

Christianity inherits the Jewish stories of exodus and exile, especially those contained in the Bible, but Christian tradition centers itself on incarnation, God becoming human, what we might even call God "migrating into history" as Jesus of Nazareth. As the epigraph on the section header reminds us, the New Testament suggests that even on earth Jesus became a migrant to Egypt as a child, though many scholars see this story more as a legend rather than a bit of actual biography. The gospels describe Jesus as itinerant, moving from place to place to preach about the reign of God, and he describes himself in Matthew and Luke as having "nowhere to lay his head" (Matt 8:20; Luke 9:58). In Christian tradition, Jesus journeys through death and returns transformed in the resurrection. Those who follow him hope for the same migrant journey, and Christians see themselves as on a journey of faith in this world, passing through on the way to their true home in God's reign, where "God [will] be all in all" (1 Cor 15:28). In ancient times, the Christian faith spread quickly as migrants and travelers carried it across the Middle East, India, Africa, and the Mediterranean. The earliest followers of Jesus were said to have died far from their homes. It is no surprise that the Church itself is described as a pilgrim or migrant on a journey. Yet more conservative Christians in modern times sometimes associate tolerant attitudes toward migrants with secular ideals of multiculturalism, which they contest in their fight against a liberal secular order.

Muslims conceive of the revelation of God in the Qur'an as a culmination of the long journey of humanity in search of God. Not surprisingly, Islamic views of migration are powerfully shaped by the life of its central prophet, Muhammad, and the foundational experiences of the early Muslim community (or *ummah*). The escape of Muhammad and the early community from the trading capital of Mecca, whose leaders rejected his monotheistic message, is almost as paradigmatic to Islam as the exodus is to Judaism. This *hijra* (journey or migration) is described by the Muslim scholar Hussam Timani not simply as story but as a teaching or doctrine. Migration has a purifying effect on migrants as they let go of attachments, but the Qur'an also suggests it is a duty when one is oppressed or unable to practice one's faith.[2] In general, Islam also looks favorably on refugees, especially those who flee to protect their community and faith. Religion scholar Amir Hussain draws attention to the role of refugees in foundational Islamic stories, including that of the initial *hijra* of those most vulnerable to persecution in Mecca, whom Muhammad sent to Abyssinia, where a Christian king welcomed them. There is also the story of Ishmael's mother, Hagar, a slave and refugee who is mother of the Prophet Muhammad's lineage.[3]

Like Christianity, Islamic theology regards human life as temporary, even fleeting, and all humans are in a real sense migrants on the earth.[4] Also like Christianity, Islam spread very quickly across cultures. The *ummah*, or Muslim community, is a global, multicultural community, a reality perhaps most powerfully experienced in the Hajj, the pilgrimage to Mecca that Muslims make at least once in their lives if they are financially able. While Judaism and Christianity speak of all human beings created in the divine image, a reality that excludes oppressive actions toward any human being, including migrants, Islam sees each human being as created with divine spirit within us, a *khalifa*, or vicegerent (representative), of God in the world. This also precludes mistreatment of migrants, whose bodies are considered sacred.[5]

The modern experience of European colonialism in traditional Muslim lands has complicated matters. On the one hand, European influence introduced secular political traditions that came to emphasize multicultural and multireligious tolerance. The sting of domination, however, has also animated a political Islam more skeptical of the place of immigrants or even longtime residents from other religious groups. Even beyond political Islam, there is controversy about the right of Muslims to migrate to majority non-Muslim lands. Muhammad Shafiq argues that Muslim law must be interpreted to allow for this if such places allow freedom of religion. He believes that Muslim scholars who oppose this do not sufficiently take into account either the human rights of the modern West or the way Western colonialism broke down the political integrity of Islamic states.[6]

Islam, Christianity, and Judaism have migration stories at the heart of their foundations. As for the religions with roots in South Asia, this is less clear. The foundations of Hinduism are difficult to parse out, being many and complex, and almost all Hindu holy sites remain within modern India. Jain origins are lost in the mists of history. Buddhism has definite origins in the decision of the Gautama Buddha, or Shakyamuni, to leave his family and home in search of enlightenment, but his story does not explicitly speak of crossing borders or journeying to new cultures. Sikhism seems to have originated in the Punjab region of India and Pakistan, and that remains its heartland. In the contemporary world, however, each of these traditions includes migrants who have journeyed far and who have made another land their permanent home. These diasporic communities reflect on the meaning and value of their journeys. We had best not discount emerging theologies of migration from their midst.

Still, the three Abrahamic religions have undeniable strong connections to foundational stories of migration. From here on, however, we focus our attention on the Christian tradition, though we will begin by tracing its shared origins with Judaism in what Christians call the Old Testament and Jews call the Tanak or simply the Bible. Those combined Jewish and Christian Scriptures have much more to say about migration and migrants than many Christians know. We turn next to that story.

Chapter Six

BIBLICAL NARRATIVES OF MIGRATION

Probably like most of us, I have had many people come at me with biblical passages to persuade me that they were right. Often it was strangers attempting to proselytize me, wanting to show me that I was not really *saved* by God, but they could facilitate that if I so desired. Other times they wanted me to align my views with theirs on some political issue, on traditional gender roles, or even regarding the alleged attributes of God. Once as I stood in a hospital waiting room in Texas, a man became very animated trying to convince me, quoting biblical passages, that only people properly terrified by God would behave themselves. We agreed to disagree. Years later, I saw that the principal problems with these tirades, as with some popular Bible studies, was that the biblical references came quickly without any real background. People would rattle off verses delivered entirely out of context. Scholars call this "proof texting," that is, citing isolated Bible verses to bolster one's preselected point. Good biblical study, on the other hand, involves interpretation of texts and stories with appropriate attention to the historical, cultural, and literary context of those passages, as well as to our own different context.

Oddly, even the most devoted Christians with strong opinions on migration rarely quote the Bible in their arguments. The one exception to that rule is the use of Romans 13, and we will examine that passage presently. The lack of attention to Scripture feels strange in part because migration occurs all over the place in the Bible, in both the

Hebrew Bible (Old Testament) and the New Testament, in both stories and teaching. As the reader will recall, this book *began* with major biblical accounts of migration—the patriarch Abraham's journey, but also that of Tobit and his son Tobias, whose stories appear in the Old Testament of the Catholic and Orthodox Bibles. Good biblical study, of course, does not stop at mere familiarity with stories and texts. An honest biblical approach to migration—or to any topic—requires that we stitch together an interpretation of many related texts, including how they fit together or do not fit together. In this chapter, we begin with interpretation of certain key texts, but we will also discern patterns and trends through an examination of the biblical theologies of migration constructed by others.

MIGRATION OUT OF CONTEXT

We begin our biblical study of migration with a short primer on biblical interpretations that fall short. Two different texts are frequently used around migration, maybe more frequently than any others, one by defenders of migrants and the other by opponents. The first passage is unique to the Gospel of Matthew (25:31–46), an account of a final judgment at the end of time, and the other text is a short section about attitudes toward secular authorities from St. Paul's letter to the Romans (13:1–7). The text from Matthew is the last part of a final sermon on eschatology, that is, the fulfillment of history and culmination of salvation. Jesus offers this sermon just before his arrest and crucifixion. Our excerpt from it imagines the end of time "when the Son of Man comes in his glory" (Matt 25:31). The "Son of Man" is a title Jesus uses of himself in Matthew and Mark; it emphasizes Jesus's identification with humanity, though some also see the Son of Man as an eschatological figure of judgment derived from the Book of Daniel in the Old Testament.[1] In any case, the text portrays this Son of Man like a king on a throne judging "all the nations" (25:32). The metaphor employed is of a shepherd separating out sheep and goats, with the sheep, or the blessed, inheriting the kingdom of God and the goats, or the accursed, sent to "the eternal fire prepared for the devil and his angels" (25:41).

The criteria for judgment are the interpretive keys to the passage; the king argues that those who fed the hungry, gave drink to the thirsty, welcomed the stranger, clothed the naked, cared for the sick, and visited the imprisoned among "the least of these who are members of my family" (25:40) did those actions for him. Those who did not, failed to do so for him. Obviously, the part about welcoming the stranger (in New Testament Greek *xenos*, literally, "foreigner") makes the passage appear relevant to issues of migration, even citing an implicit divine threat against those who refuse to welcome migrants. On the one hand, this command coheres with other New Testament passages emphasizing the general duty to hospitality, as we will see below. On the other hand, the "least of these who are members of my family" appears to refer to the followers of Jesus, present and future.[2] Thus, the passage may serve exceedingly well as a message of hope to immigrant Christians suffering abuse and as a challenge to churches to welcome immigrant Christians. But it performs less well as a general biblical injunction condemning to hell all people who refuse to welcome immigrants.

Another migration text proves even more problematic. Often quoted by opponents of illegal immigration, especially purveyors of the rule of law narrative discussed in chapter 3, Romans 13:1–7 begins, "Let every person be subject to the governing authorities; for there is no authority except from God, and those authorities that exist have been instituted by God. Therefore, whoever resists authority resists what God has appointed, and those who resist will incur judgment" (13:1–2). In the summer of 2018, Attorney General Jeff Sessions invoked this passage in defending the U.S. government's "zero tolerance" policy, which sought to prosecute all adults who entered the country illegally, separating children from their parents. As was noted in media reports at the time, the passage has been cited in different ways over the centuries to defend the established social order, as when Martin Luther referred to it to justify the brutal quelling of the German Peasant Revolts of 1524 and 1525, when colonial American Loyalists quoted it to *condemn* the American Revolution, or when U.S. Southerners made reference to the passage to defend the requirement of the Fugitive Slave Act of 1850 that Northerners turn over escaped slaves to their owners.[3] In a way, it has functioned as an indispensable passage to support the existing political order when it comes under fire by Christians, especially with its clear threat of judgment by God. But is this use of the passage true to its original context?

The author of the passage, St. Paul, places it in his long letter to the Christian community at Rome, a church he had never visited. It is a kind of letter of introduction summarizing his message to a community that included many Christian Jews, some of whom may have been suspicious of Paul, the famed Jewish apostle who spent most of his time with those who were not Jewish. It occurs in a section of the letter devoted to advice for daily life, and it is followed by mention of the imminent return of Christ and the end of history. Paul clearly does *not* want Christians making legal trouble for themselves in the capital of the Roman Empire, where they have no power, where already Jews and probably Christian Jews have been expelled more than once, and especially given that Christ would return soon to make all things right. This emphasis on Christ's imminent return shapes most of St. Paul's teachings, including his strong recommendation of celibacy in 1 Corinthians 7:25–31.[4]

Given this larger context, it seems unwarranted to treat this passage as a blanket biblical injunction against disobeying the law, proof texting at its most transparent. Instead, St. Paul stakes out a claim for obedience to the law—also urging people to pay taxes, by the way, a point usually omitted by politicians quoting the passage—in particular circumstances, circumstances largely alien to our own. Most of us no longer expect an imminent end to history; we cannot afford to neglect the errors of our own government. In a democracy, at least some people do have influence over the state. Finally, Christians still constitute a majority in North America, and they are unlikely to be expelled any time soon. In short, it appears irresponsible to use this passage to justify mass deportations or to stigmatize undocumented immigrants, especially given the innumerable biblical passages about hospitality to strangers.

Unsurprisingly, other parts of the Bible offer a more ambivalent attitude toward government or political authorities. In the Hebrew Bible, prophets never tire of attacking the kings of Judah and Israel for their idolatry or unjust treatment of the poor. Jeremiah ended up in prison for this reason (Jer 37:11–16). In the New Testament, John the Baptist preached against Herod Antipas until the latter had him imprisoned and eventually beheaded. In the Gospel of Luke, Jesus's mother Mary speaks of God who "has brought down the powerful from their thrones, and lifted up the lowly" (Luke 1:52). Jesus himself dies at the hands of the Roman government, executed unjustly. Revelation 13 treats those same Roman authorities as actual agents of the devil. So clearly, the Bible's overall message is not to obey the authorities at all times. It matters whether those authorities are behaving in a just manner, and one's position in the power structure.

MIGRATION IN THE HEBREW BIBLE, OR OLD TESTAMENT

For Christians to search the Scriptures to help understand migration as a phenomenon requires an adequate understanding of the historical and cultural context of migration in the ancient world when the Bible was written. As the theologian Peter Phan notes, ancient migration was primarily driven by three major factors: war, trade, and nomadism.[5] We might also add famine, which, for example, brought Jacob's sons into Egypt in search of food (Gen 42:1–5).[6] War often involved mass deportations and exile as punishments for peoples who resisted imperial ambitions, a fate that the Northern Kingdom of Israel and the Southern Kingdom of Judah suffered in the Bible. War and trade brought people across great distances, drawn by soldiering and plunder or by making a living as a traveling merchant. Nomadic peoples largely made a living by herding animals; they needed to move where the wild grains were plentiful, careful not to overgraze. Thus, while Abraham leaves home because he is called by God, much of his subsequent movement seems driven by the need for good pastureland. All this is to say that migration in the ancient world was common.

Because it was common, and because travel was not necessarily safe—thieves and raiders could act with impunity in the spaces between governments—hospitality became a matter of life and death. The story of Abraham welcoming God's messengers in Genesis 18:1–15 and the warning in Hebrews 13:2 to welcome strangers, since they may be angels in disguise, both match up with many stories in ancient mythology about the reward or punishment doled out to those who welcome or refuse to welcome gods traveling incognito. The Abraham story adds the additional layer that God's message comes to those who welcome his messenger; those who do not offer hospitality to the stranger or who will not listen to the stranger do not receive God's message.[7]

On the other hand, in spite of all this movement, for the agricultural society of the ancient biblical world, land was wealth. This made those who had no land or no one to work the land, such as widows and orphans, vulnerable to poverty or exploitation by others. Often grouped together with widows and orphans in the Hebrew Bible are the "resident aliens," in Hebrew *gerim*, essentially immigrants or refugees, as distinguished from those who were passing through, often for reasons of trade without intending to stay, the *nokrim*. "The noun *ger*...likely refers to a person of foreign origin who migrates into Israel because of war, famine, poverty, impending debt slavery or the like. He will typically be a person who has come to stay in Israel and to become part of the Israelite society."[8] Again, it should be noted that the presence of *gerim* is not seen as exceptional or rare, a point echoed by the large numbers in King Solomon's census of immigrant residents (1 Chr 2:16–17), though like most numbers in the Bible, it is undoubtedly an exaggeration. In any case, because neither *gerim* nor *nokrim* could own Israelite land, the former as permanent settlers lived at the mercy of Israelites.[9]

Consequently, in passages throughout the first five books of the Bible, the Torah or Pentateuch, God issues strongly worded commands regarding the *gerim*—like Israelites they are to be loved and not oppressed (Exod 22:21; Lev 19:33–34; 24:22; Deut 10:18–19); they are to be under the same laws as Israelites (Exod 12:49; Lev 24:22; Num 9:14; 15:15–16; Deut 1:16); immigrant workers possess rights (Deut 24:14); and agricultural leftovers are to be offered to them as they are for vulnerable widows and orphans (Lev 19:9–10; 23:22; Deut 24:19–22). In a large number of these passages, the command is preceded or followed by a reminder that the Israelites themselves were strangers or immigrants in Egypt. The dark memory of oppression in a foreign land should motivate better treatment by Israelites of the foreigners in their midst. As we will see, some biblical theologians make explicit parallels to immigrant nations today, where citizens' treatment of migrants seems shaped by how they have forgotten that their own ancestors were immigrants.[10]

Many passages in the prophetic books echo these commands in the Torah (see, e.g., Isa 16:4; Jer 7:5–7; 22:3–5; Ezek 47:21–22; Zech 7:8–10). There are also various biblical tales of virtuous immigrants, both Israelites in the Diaspora, such as our friend from the first chapter, Tobit, and immigrants to Israel. Among them, Ruth, a Moabite who follows her mother-in-law, Naomi, to Israel after her husband's death, is raised up as the very paradigm of fidelity. Some scholars, however, have criticized the way Ruth appears to easily discard her own culture and people to enthusiastically embrace Israelite ways, as if it were that simple, as if everyone agreed on the cultural superiority of Israel. Yet biblical scholar Anne-Marie Schol-Wetter suggests that Ruth's story tells us something more: "She displays a loyalty (*hesed*) that reaches across the apparently unbridgeable divide between 'Israel' and 'Moab.'"[11] Her story reminds us that cultural identity is never so one-sided or simple.

Of course, not all foreigners appear this virtuous in the Hebrew Bible, and not all biblical writers have laudatory views of foreigners. Deuteronomy and Joshua, for example, contain some disturbing divine instructions regarding the wanton destruction of Canaanite towns and cities, including putting all the inhabitants to the sword (see Deut 20:16–18), though these are delivered in the context of war and conquest rather than everyday interaction with immigrants. Particularly in texts assembled after the Babylonian exile, there is concern about the negative influence of foreigners, especially foreign spouses, on the fidelity of Israelites to their covenant with God (see 1 Kgs 11:1–13; Neh 13:23–27). In a kind of reversal of the memory commands in the Torah enjoining mercy on the immigrant, the author of Psalm 137 not only pledges from exile in Babylon to never forget the cruelty of the Chaldeans toward the Judeans but also blesses whatever future warrior shall wipe that people out, dashing their children's heads against the rocks (Ps 137:8–9)! While these passages are more lament or warning than commandment, and more attuned to dangerous than settled times, they remind us that the Bible is not protected from the very human fear of the stranger.

MIGRATION IN THE NEW TESTAMENT

Like the Hebrew Bible, the New Testament recognizes the way strangers or immigrants can be instruments of God's interventions or divine messengers. When Jesus finds that a group of Greeks have approached Philip wanting to see him, he sees this as a sign that the hour of his death and resurrection is near (John 12:20–24). Both a Syro-Phoenician, or Canaanite, woman (Mark 7:24–30; Matt 15:21–28) and a Roman centurion (Matt 8:5–13; Luke 7:1–10) surprise Jesus with their faith in him. Another centurion, Cornelius, receives a vision from God that persuades the apostle Peter to baptize him and his household (Acts 10). Clearly, the New Testament follows patterns in the Old Testament by which the foreigner turns out to be the one expressing or living God's Word. The Good Samaritan, a foreigner, serves as an example of God's mercy in Luke 10:29–37.

We should also note, however, how all of these episodes are shaped by the writers' knowledge that faith in Jesus would soon spread across cultural and political boundaries. The followers of Jesus would end up as more than a reform movement among Palestinian Jews, as Jesus seems to have first understood them. The resulting multicultural church was symbolized by the Pentecost (Acts 2:1–41), where the apostles spoke in their own language (Aramaic) but were heard in countless languages by a multilingual crowd. This is not to say that community across cultures always proceeded smoothly. In Acts 6:1–7, it emerges that in the Jerusalem community Aramaic-speaking widows were receiving preferential treatment over Greek-speaking widows with cultural-linguistic roots outside Palestine. Much of the content of the letters of St. Paul deals with controversies over how much of Jewish law non-Jewish converts needed to observe.

Even so, the Christian community's rapid movement across borders and boundaries was astonishing. Just in the New Testament, we see explicit and implicit references to Christians in Samaria (John 4:4–42; Acts 8:4–24), Ethiopia (Acts 8:26–39), and Cyrene in North Africa (Mark 15:21), and in Acts and the letters of St. Paul, references to Christians in Syria, Asia Minor (Turkey), Greece, and Rome itself. We hear mention of many itinerant souls who traveled sharing the message about Jesus, not just St. Paul, but the apostle Peter, Barnabas, the couple Prisca and Aquila, Timothy, Epaphroditus, and countless others. Within the Church, there were no more strangers or foreigners but only "citizens with the saints and also members of the household of God" (Eph 2:19). By the time the Book of Revelation was written in the late first century, the prophet John could envision the Christian faithful as "a great multitude that no one could count, from every nation, from all tribes and peoples and languages" (Rev 7:9). While none of this may seem to deal directly with migration, it affirms that early Christians saw migration and movement as natural, often in the service of Christ, and that from early on they saw their community as one that embraced many peoples and cultures united in one baptism and faith. This should lead Christians to ask questions about the legitimacy of cultural narratives of migration that presume ethnic or national boundaries matter more than anything else.

BIBLICAL THEOLOGIES OF MIGRATION

Many Christians (and non-Christians) assume that religious teaching is ordinarily univocal, that is, always speaks with a singular voice. Thus do Evangelical Christians begin by asking, "What does the Bible say?" and Catholic Christians often begin by asking, "What does the Church teach?" It should be clear by now that biblical teaching comes to us with many voices, each shaped by particular historical circumstances, the dilemmas of Israel and of Jesus's disciples in different eras. Israel's attitudes toward foreigners in general shifts depending on its history, and Jesus's disciples were focused on sharing the message about him across cultures, though the crossing of cultural boundaries sometimes also created unusual and new problems. So how, then, are people to make sense of biblical stories and teaching that relate to migration in our own time? The answer, clearly, is in different ways.

This is not to say that Christians may interpret the Bible any way they please. While some U.S. Christians insist that their nation has no responsibility for outsiders suffering violence or persecution (68 percent of white Evangelical Christians and 45 percent of Catholics, according to a recent poll[12]), this position is clearly at odds with New Testament teaching emphasizing love of neighbor, which extends even to enemies. Nevertheless, within the boundaries of biblical thinking on the subject of migration, there is much diversity. Here I will present the thinking of four different biblical scholars: one a Catholic, two Evangelical Christians with competing views, and the third a liberal Protestant.

The Catholic scholar Donald Senior, CP, was president of the Catholic Theological Union (CTU) in Chicago for twenty-three years, where he taught New Testament. CTU is a seminary and theological graduate school founded by multiple Catholic religious orders that educates priests in formation, religious sisters, and lay Christians from all over the world. Senior edited the Catholic Study Bible and was on the Vatican's Pontifical Biblical Commission. He affirms a point already made, that migration is woven into a very large number of biblical stories and events, from the exodus to Jesus's own itinerary. As to the theological implications of all this, Senior focuses on the New Testament, and he argues that Jesus's itinerancy emphasizes his solidarity with the marginalized and oppressed, including many migrants and refugees today. Jesus's followers created a community always in tension with the human desire to idolize security and stability and to focus on the accumulation of material goods. Christians should be, to a certain extent, exiles and strangers in a world that emphasizes these things, set upon their ultimate destiny in heaven.[13]

Senior also draws our attention to a fundamental value and practice of the New Testament—hospitality. Emerging from the Old Testament commands regarding the stranger, hospitality is seen as a basic responsibility of the Christian leader in the New Testament. To Senior, the deeper reason for this gradually dawns on the first apostles and leaders: the message of Jesus is meant for all people, for the whole world. "Welcoming the stranger is not simply an act of kindness and solidarity....The stranger who migrates across one's borders is also a sign of the full scope of the human family, a scope that, within the New Testament vision, transcends bloodlines and national boundaries."[14] No particular family, ethnic group, or nation has a monopoly on God's mercy and salvation, and hospitality to the stranger is the demonstration par excellence of this truth. According to this conception, Christians should not use hospitality instrumentally, as a kind of carrot to draw people into the faith or into the pews. Instead, "the biblical vision of the human family as one before God" means that Christians cannot tolerate racial or nationalistic superiority, the absolutizing of borders or boundaries, or the denial of anyone's dignity or rights because they do not come from one's own people or land.[15] Though Senior does not spell them out, that has significant consequences for immigration policy and practice.

Evangelical Christian biblical scholar and archaeologist James K. Hoffmeier is more willing to state the practical contemporary consequences of his reading of the Bible on migration. Hoffmeier makes a biblical argument for the legitimacy of a strict moral line between immigrants with legal papers and those without, the perspective espoused in the rule of law narrative in chapter 3. His view, like that of certain Evangelical politicians, stems in part from a strict interpretation of Romans 13. Christians must obey the law, even laws they consider unjust.[16] But Hoffmeier also insists that the Hebrew term *ger*, usually translated as *resident alien*, is equivalent today to immigrants with legal status only. The strong biblical protections toward the *gerim* in the Torah, in Hoffmeier's view, do not apply at all to unauthorized immigrants.[17] Citing the granting and also denial of permission to cross borders in ancient Egypt and in the stories of various biblical figures in the Torah, or Pentateuch, and noting a general ancient respect for property rights, Hoffmeier concludes that ancient biblical migrants could not settle anywhere without local permission, which he then connects with a permanent visa—in the United States, a green card today. Unauthorized immigrants, he suggests, should be compared to more transient visitors like the *nokhrim*, who had fewer rights.[18]

There are problems with this logic. Hoffmeier posits that the difference between the more protected resident aliens (*gerim*) and the temporary sojourners with fewer rights (*nokhrim*) lies primarily in their legal status, not in their intended length of stay, as other scholars argued above. This seems to project back into the Bible and the ancient world very modern notions of citizenship or legal status. The boundaries of ancient kingdoms and empires were established by armies, not by treaties or agreements, and people's loyalties were often to their town or tribe.[19] Hoffmeier rightly asserts that ancient borders were patrolled, that transit papers were issued, and that people could be "deported," but much of this was opportunistic and ad hoc. No government had the omnipresent administrative reach of the modern nation-state, and most people had no documentation that they existed at all. The world was not divided into clear national units; only elites had any recognized rights at all. All this makes it very difficult to posit that the distinguishing characteristic of the *gerim* was their legal status.

The Old Testament scholar M. Daniel Carroll R., also an Evangelical Christian, comes to very different conclusions about Romans 13 and the laws protecting the *gerim*. A seminary professor in Denver and Guatemala City, Carroll, a Guatemalan American, has a particular concern for Hispanic Christians in the United States. Carroll begins with the first chapter of Genesis, where God creates human beings in the divine image and likeness, which he sees as counterpoint not only to migration-induced feelings of shame or inferiority but also to the reactive desire of some immigrants to belittle the culture or people of their adoptive land.[20] Like Senior, he points to biblical figures on the move at different points for different reasons. He emphasizes the complex biblical accounts of migration and exile as "a divine mirror, where they [immigrants today] see themselves."[21] Carroll tackles the Torah laws on *gerim*, noting in them a counterexample to the oppression the Israelites experienced in Egypt. For Israel, God's law was meant to direct them and serve as a paradigm, to be an example to other states and cultures. Therefore, Carroll sees the command to care for these strangers as binding on Christians today, and native-born Americans, like the ancient Israelites, should recognize that their identity is bound up in their own immigrant past and present. Carroll also sees the integration of the *gerim* into Israel as a call for new immigrants to respect the cultures in their new land and to make efforts to learn American ways.[22]

Carroll's treatment of the New Testament does not add much to his overall argument, except to recognize Jesus's abiding concern for outsiders in his own society, from Samaritans to tax collectors to lepers.[23] He does address, however, a passage that many of his fellow Evangelicals use to criticize undocumented immigrants, Romans 13. Relying on this passage alone, he notes, ignores the responsibility Christians have even to their enemies (Matt 5:43–48). But Carroll does not feel, as a Christian who holds to biblical inerrancy, that he can just dismiss the passage: "Of course, there would be those who set aside the passage on exegetical, theological, and pastoral grounds. My experience, however, is with Hispanic Christians primarily of the evangelical and Pentecostal streams. They would take this biblical text seriously, but their view is complex."[24] He helpfully notes that the passage counsels *submission* though not necessarily obedience to authorities; laws considered unjust or inadequate to human needs can and should be changed. The passage also follows Romans 12, where Christians are exhorted not to be shaped by the expectations of their culture or nation. Undocumented immigrant Christians, he argues, recognize both that they have violated the law and that the law is far from perfect and requires reform.[25]

Ched Myers is a mainline Protestant biblical scholar and social justice activist from Berkeley. He is most well known for a powerfully written political account of the Gospel of Mark, *Binding the Strong Man*, which identifies the demonic with the oppressive Roman Empire.[26] Like others, Myers begins with the biblical notion of hospitality, even making reference to Old Testament cities of refuge, where criminal perpetrators could flee for asylum while awaiting trial. If God too appears as a vulnerable stranger in need of hospitality, as in Genesis 18, but also in Jesus becoming human, then God himself is a kind

106

of immigrant or refugee, and in Myers's view not one with allegiance to any particular state or government: "The God of the Bible is consistently portrayed as 'stateless,' and we can reasonably add *undocumented*. This is in stark contrast to the patron-gods of the empires that surround Israel, who lived comfortably in the temples of the king."[27] He relates this to Jesus's itineracy, even picking up on Pastor Bob Eckblad's notion of Jesus as the *buen coyote*, the good smuggler, who transits sinners who by their own merits have no right to the reign of God, as opposed to the ruthless ones we sometimes see.[28]

The second half of Myers's deliberately provocative argument in favor of hospitality to immigrants, including undocumented immigrants, recounts an episode from the Book of Judges. A man from the tribe of Ephraim is denied hospitality by local residents in a town of the tribe of Benjamin. But his own countryman, an immigrant resident in the village, does welcome him (Judg 19:15–21). Myers then points to how Americans, like the Israelites, should know better, remembering their own immigrant pasts and in empathy offering hospitality. Forgetting enables cold-heartedness that gives space to cultural narratives that see immigrants, or even just undocumented immigrants, as a threat. "At the point one's immigrant narrative has been erased, as has happened with most European Americans in the United States," he concludes, "there is no point of contact to constrain the development of beliefs that the 'door should be closed' to those now perceived as too different, threating, or burdensome."[29]

But Myers then continues to analyze the story in Judges, which takes a dreadful turn. Local residents violently attack the host's house, resulting in the rape and grisly death of the traveler's "concubine"—more like what we would call a cohabitating partner—which in turn sets off a fratricidal war among the Israelite tribes in which Benjamin is nearly wiped out entirely (Judg 20:1—21:25). Myers sees this as a kind of political parable or cautionary tale. Denying hospitality to strangers because they are strangers inevitably opens up space for violence against them, violence that eventually envelops everyone.[30] Many readers may find Myers's provocative approach and choice of biblical texts off-putting, but his point about the connection between forgetting one's past and a lack of empathy and hospitality remains. And it is hard not to look at the history of nativist violence in American history, including in more recent times, and not worry just a little bit about the cost of inciting hatred of immigrants, with or without legal papers.

SACRED NARRATIVES AND MIGRATION

For many Christians, these biblical theologies of migration, controversial or not, do not serve as the final word of guidance as to the place of immigrants in contemporary society or how we should view the different cultural narratives about migration. Biblical teaching serves more as a foundation, the beginning of a long process of community reflection across history. Christians have never stopped thinking about the place of migration and migrants in the everyday life of believers or in God's plan. For Catholics, Orthodox Christians, and a good number of Protestants, reflection on the biblical texts is only the beginning of a theology of migration. We turn next to the development of theological thinking on migration across Christian history.

Section Four

THEOLOGICAL NARRATIVES AND MIGRATION

Let all guests who arrive be received like Christ....In the salutation of all guests, whether arriving or departing, let all humility be shown. Let the head be bowed or the whole body prostrated on the ground in adoration of Christ, who indeed is received in their persons.

—Rule of St. Benedict[1]

Chapter Seven

MIGRATION IN CHRISTIAN HISTORY AND TRADITION

Christians who put stock in the ongoing, centuries-long process of reflection on God's plan for humanity refer to that process as *tradition* (a Latin translation of the Greek *paradosis*, implying a handing over of precious things). In previous eras, people sometimes thought about tradition as definitive, unchanging teachings passed down from the distant past. But tradition is really more like a very long and oft-changing conversation that people keep joining and then leaving but where some of the best insights of the conversations are recorded along the way. Lucretia Yaghjian reminds us that the conversation can get heated,[2] but perhaps unlike many arguments in our families or among our friends, the conversation does not stop just because one party stomps off.

Christians will sometimes value certain strands of the conversation that is tradition more highly than others, even focusing on a handful of thinkers in a particular historical epoch. All Christians privilege the tradition conversation as it unfolded in the first century of Christian life, especially those voices that came to be included in the New Testament. But Orthodox Christians, for example, also pay a great deal of attention to some of the big thinkers of the first seven or eight centuries, the patristic era, so named after these "Church fathers" (there were also mothers, but fewer of them were remembered in writing). Especially in the nineteenth and twentieth centuries, Catholics valued theological conversations from the Middle Ages very highly, usually including Thomas

Aquinas and often in contradistinction to more modern thinkers whom they viewed as dangerous at that time. Protestants, not surprisingly, put emphasis on the Reformers of the sixteenth century—John Calvin, Martin Luther, Thomas Cromwell, Menno Simons, and others. In recent years, Christians across the spectrum seem more willing to listen to contemporary voices, even sometimes those of secular people and non-Christian religious thinkers.

For our purposes here, I try to take seriously the full scope of theological teaching and reflection on migration across these different time periods. Rather than focus on particular thinkers in detail, I will offer a broad swath of thinking on migration and migrants. In the last chapter, we saw how migration emerged as a topic in the Jewish and Christian Bibles, usually pointing people toward compassion and hospitality for migrants, since many of the key biblical figures were migrants themselves. As the universal mission of Christianity becomes apparent in New Testament times, hospitality to migrants becomes a symbol of that universality. Those themes grow in importance throughout the patristic era, though they are reshaped into elite practices due to a radical change of social and political conditions during the European Middle Ages. After the Protestant Reformation, the modern era begins with the rise of the very nation-states that accept and restrict migrants today. The Enlightenment, the most influential theological movement of the modern period in Europe, turned many of those nation-states into constitutional states with laws and borders, not only in Europe but around the world. It did so through colonization, a key part of new waves of global migration in the modern era, waves also set in motion by global capitalism. Christian communities today continue to wrestle with migration as it is shaped by all of these factors—nation-states, laws and borders, colonialism and decolonization, global capitalism. As in the Bible itself, the conclusions Christians have drawn about these matters are not monolithic or univocal, but patterns can be discerned.

ITINERANT CHRISTIANITY IN THE EARLY YEARS

As we already saw in our exploration of the Bible, migration played a significant role in the ancient world, and this includes during the early years of Christianity. The theologian Peter Phan points out that much secular scholarship on migration tends to focus on the modern era, beginning with the stirrings of European colonialism in the sixteenth century, even though migration is as old as the human race.[3] Early Christianity's itinerary—its migrant nature—is perhaps best related in a little-known story about the coming of Christianity. Much of the story comes from the Xi'an monument erected in the eighth century (and then rediscovered in the seventeenth century) outside of the ancient Chinese capital of Xi'an, though other texts confirm the story. The monument tells of the arrival of a Syriac-speaking priest by the name of Aluoben in 635. Officially received by Chinese authorities, his arrival occasioned a kind of edict that allowed for Christianity to spread in China. All this suggests that Christianity first came to China via Silk Road merchants and that enough influential locals had embraced Christianity that a priest was requested and the emperor was persuaded to make space for it. Aluoben seems to have learned Chinese and both wrote and translated texts promoting monotheism in China.[4]

This story provides some contrast with a more romantic view that the early disciples of Jesus wandered the world in search of foreign people with whom to share the message about Jesus. Some certainly did, and the peripatetic life of St. Paul and certain stories in the Acts of the Apostles, such as the odd tale of Philip being teleported into the presence of an Ethiopian court official in Acts 8:26–39, lend credence to this view. After the New Testament, there arose a plethora of stories and legends about the wanderings of the original apostles and some of their companions. A closer inspection of these stories, however, shows that the emphasis was more on the miraculous power of God in the life of the missionary and teacher than on the romance of wandering and travel.[5] Picturing the early Christians as imbued with missionary wanderlust is perhaps more a projection backward from the modern missionary movement of the sixteenth to twentieth centuries.

Rather than being rooted in missionary romance, the itineracy of the early Christians depended on all the other social factors that encouraged migration in the ancient world. First, the Jewish Diaspora enabled the spread of what was, in the beginning, a Jewish movement. It is no accident that early Christianity ended up in cities like Antioch in Syria, Alexandria in Egypt, and Rome itself; these cities retained large Jewish populations. In fact, there were far more Jews outside of Palestine in that era than inside Roman-occupied Judea and Galilee.

After a revolt in 70 CE, Jerusalem and its temple were destroyed by the Romans, and this and other Roman reprisals undoubtedly led to the exile of those Christians who identified as Jews.[6] But while political expulsions played a role in the spread of early Christianity (see, e.g., Acts 18:2–3), other factors like trade, famine, slave trafficking, and economic migration probably played an even greater role. The extensive road system within the Roman Empire, kept safe for the transport of troops, the Silk Road that transported traders to Central Asia, and extensive shipping routes throughout the Mediterranean and into the Indian Ocean facilitated the movement of Christian migrants, including the merchants and priest Aluoben that brought Christianity to China. The strength of regional languages—Aramaic and later Syriac in the Middle East; koine Greek in the eastern Mediterranean; and Latin in the western Mediterranean—also helped Christians to settle somewhere else more easily.

As the tale of Aluoben indicates, Christianity spread far beyond the Roman Empire, where it eventually became the de facto official religion. Within a century or two, Christians lived in Syria, Mesopotamia (now Iraq), and Persia (Iran). The initial migrants that brought the faith to these areas held to Palestinian Jewish customs, but they later adapted their Christianity to Syrian culture and the Syriac language, and Syrian Christianity then spread to India, Central Asia, and eventually even China by the seventh century. In Persia, Syrian Christian worship and customs took on the Persian language and culture, until the rise of Islam turned Persian Christians back to their Syrian roots. In China, Syrian culture never departed, although archaeological finds like the Xi'an monument demonstrate the attempts made by Christians to defend their faith in the Confucian idiom of Chinese society.[7] Christian migrants from Egypt made their way south into Sudan and Ethiopia and west into Roman North Africa. Roman Christians also traveled through what is today Spain, France, Germany, and the British Isles. Irenaeus, a Christian bishop who led the community in present-day Lyons, France, originally hailed from the Greek city of Smyrna, located in present-day Turkey.[8]

The itinerant nature of early Christianity produced migrant-friendly church structures and strong customs of hospitality. The late first-century *Didache*, an instruction for baptism and church life, demands that Christians respect the authority of itinerant preachers and leaders, even though they were strangers to the community. These visiting teachers,

114

apostles, or prophets were to be welcomed like Christ, and they should be permitted to teach or speak God's Word to the community. Even after this itinerant leadership class declined, Christian communities maintained elaborate lists of the distant communities with whom they shared the bond of faith. Bishops exchanged letters; and traveling Christians, often bringing pieces of the eucharistic bread from their home church, were offered hospitality. This is not to say that there were no limits to such hospitality. The *Didache* recommends that if visiting prophets or apostles stay too long or require donations, they should immediately be sent on their way. One can easily imagine an enterprising stranger posing as a prophet and then summarily being tossed out of town once he started "borrowing" money from hospitable listeners.[9]

Itineracy shaped the very metaphors by which Christians understood their tribe. Patristic Christians thought of themselves as strangers or immigrants in the world. Intermittent persecutions heightened this sense of transient belonging. The *Letter to Diognetus* from this period describes Christians thus: "[Christians] live in their native countries, but only as outsiders. They participate in everything like citizens and tolerate all things as foreigners. Every foreign place is their homeland, and every homeland is foreign."[10] As strangers and outsiders in this world, Christians felt solidarity with literal outsiders, and so they would distribute money to needy migrants. The Cappadocian bishop and theologian Basil and his sister Macrina built hostels to house strangers. "Whom do we harm," Basil wrote to a hesitant Roman governor, "by building a place of hospitality for strangers?"[11] Even as monks and nuns began to retreat from the world to work and pray, they incorporated a house for guests in their monasteries (ironically, Western monks did so even as they took vows of stability that prevented them from moving around). As Peter Phan notes, despite this impressive commitment to hospitality, welcome was not extended to everyone. Amid the sibling rivalry between Christians and Jews, Christians could be cavalier and even cruel to migrant Jews.[12]

PENITENTS AND PILGRIMS

Even as Christian communities grew more rooted and stable during the early centuries of the faith, itineracy—real and imagined, past and present—generated a kind of transient theology of human life. Human beings were never quite at home in this world, never still in their journey toward God. Even when the erratic persecutions of Christians ended and Christianity allied itself with various Near Eastern kingdoms and with the Roman imperial state, heroic restlessness drove some out into the desert to live as monks or hermits. Especially in the Eastern Roman, or Byzantine, Empire, liturgy and worship came to be seen as a kind of temporary celestial migration by which ordinary Christians found their way to divine transformation, or *theosis*. The rural and urban monasteries of Eastern Christianity gave rise to a new sense of interior wandering, a mystical spirituality of movement toward divine union.[13] The image of the Christian as stranger or migrant upon the earth shifted to an image of the Christian as an ascending soul.

Meanwhile, the great empires of antiquity began to fall, and the outward stability of economic and political life could no longer be taken for granted. The rise of Islam created a persistent threat to the Byzantine Empire, and Islamic empires cut off communication between Christians in Europe and minority Christian communities across the Middle East, in Central and South Asia, and in Africa. Early medieval Europe entered a period dominated by marauding invaders, competing warlords, and kings and emperors who maintained power by managing the chaos. By the tenth century in Europe, however, the warlord era came to an end, and a new political and economic system arose, centered on local estates, managed by nobles, and worked by serfs bound to the land.[14] Western Christians in particular began to imagine themselves not as immigrants on the earth or ascending souls but as subjects of Christendom, an interconnected network of territories drawn together by allegiance to the papacy and the Catholic Church.

Geographical movement became less a metaphor for the faith journey and more a purposeful act with either a practical or spiritual purpose. On a more practical level, a small clergy elite circulated around Europe for diplomatic or educational reasons. The monks of Cluny established a network of monasteries around Europe. A thirteenth-century Italian Dominican like Thomas Aquinas could journey to Paris to study and teach and find himself living and working in essentially the same Latin-speaking clerical culture as in Rome or Naples. But medieval people also set off for more romantic reasons. Irish monks drifted off to found monasteries wherever the current would take them.[15] Francis of Assisi journeyed to Egypt with his mind set on converting the sultan, the Islamic leader, to Christianity (he failed to do so). Soldiers enlisted in the Christian forces of the various crusades, though killing in war was also seen as such a grievous sin that it often required a dramatic act of penance, such as pilgrimage to a far-off shrine. Not all pilgrims journeyed to such shrines to expiate their sins, but nearly all traveled simply, dependent on local hospitality. Hospitality remained as a Christian ideal but was addressed more to elites than to ordinary Christians.

NEW WORLDS AND NATION-STATES

By the sixteenth century, European Christians began to lay the foundations for much of the world of migration that we encounter. The feudal order of nobles and serfs, bishops and pope, gave way to a new urban economy of trade and the local production of goods. The growth of the economy in towns and cities led to migration, both within and across regions. Significant populations from other parts of Europe settled in major urban centers, and not merely students and clergy. Even as early as 1215, the Fourth Lateran Council of the Catholic Church noted and made pastoral provision for the new arrivals:

> Since in many places within the same city and diocese there are people of different languages having one faith but various rites and customs, we strictly command that the bishops of these cities and dioceses provide suitable men who will, according to the different rites and languages, celebrate the divine offices for them, administer the sacraments of the Church, and instruct them by word and example.[16]

The new economy eventually led to the creation of city-states in some parts of Europe (e.g., Italy), regional principalities in others (e.g., Germany), and centralized nation-states in still other parts of Europe (e.g., France and England). In 1492, the Catholic rulers of Spain defeated the remnant of al-Andalus in Granada, the last outpost of the Muslim kingdom of Spain. The same rulers demanded that remaining Jews and Muslims either convert or leave, centering Spanish identity on Catholic faith.

Various European kings orchestrated a similar process of cultural and religious homogenization. In 1539, for example, the king of France made Parisian French the national language, displacing regional dialects. The persistence of regional cultures and religious diversity even to this day shows that such efforts were not entirely successful, but they nonetheless planted in the minds of Europeans the idea that a nation-state should correspond to a single culture insulated by its territorial borders. This conception of the nation-state became a structural reality in Europe with the end of the so-called Wars of Religion of the Reformation. The wars were as much about competing national identities and power as they were about competing Catholic and Protestant Christianity. The Peace of Augsburg (1555) and of Westphalia (1648) organized Europe so that each king or prince had supreme authority with more or less clear territorial boundaries.[17]

Perhaps the most disturbing conflict between emerging nation-states and migrants in early modern Europe was the battle between state authorities and itinerant Roma people, popularly known today as Gypsies, then oddly known as Egyptians, though no one really thought they were from Egypt. They were actually from northwest India. After the fall of the Byzantine Empire to the Turks in the fifteenth century, Roma began to migrate across Europe, many converting to Christianity in the process. Various groups either received or forged papers declaring that they were pilgrims entitled to protection, and that initially seems to have been successful. Over time, however, matters shifted. A population boom, coupled with crop failures, increased poverty to such an extent that the traditional charity of the Church for migrants was overwhelmed. As nation-states became more powerful and centralized, they developed tighter notions of what it meant to be a subject. Suspicion of "foreigners" increased. By the sixteenth century, both Spain and England criminalized and attempted to expel the Roma, including those who had been born locally.[18]

This increasingly taken-for-granted notion of nation-states, including cultural and religious homogenization, clear boundaries, and the centralization of power spread throughout the world, though it required several centuries to do so. One of the principal agents of that spread was European colonialism. Nation-states not only had power and resources to wage war and conduct authoritative diplomacy but also could equip and authorize the conquest of territory. Spain and Portugal conquered much of the Americas and the Philippines even as the Reformation unfolded in Europe, and Portugal established coastal trading stations in Africa, India, and beyond. England and France eventually established their own colonies. The resulting demographic disaster in the Americas—millions died of European diseases—along with the Catholic condemnation of indigenous slavery, created a demand for laborers. The mother countries required their raw materials, and the brutal, emerging Atlantic slave trade provided the labor. In this way, colonization of the Americas created perhaps the most colossal and one of the most disruptive waves of migration in human history, both voluntary and compulsory.

This colonization also reignited a romantic notion of Christian itineracy, first among Catholics and then later among Protestants. Among Catholics, a new ideal of missionary sacrifice centered on religious orders like the Dominicans, Franciscans, and Jesuits, first men and then later religious sisters. Some of these missionaries worked hard to acquire the languages and to understand the cultures of the indigenous people they hoped to bring to the faith. Others simply complained that their romantic dreams of mass conversion came to nothing, often blaming the very people they claimed to love.[19] A few missionaries, such as the Spanish Dominicans Antonio de Montesinos and Bartolomé de Las Casas, stepped forward to defend the rights of indigenous people, threatening the Spanish governors and landlords with hellfire. In a letter to the Royal Council of Indies, Las Casas finishes his argument against Spanish tyranny by asserting, "The Indian nations have the right, which will be theirs till the Day of Judgment, to make just war against us and erase us from the face of the earth."[20]

Montesinos and Las Casas witnessed the very beginning of the gradual and often violent process of the mixing of peoples and cultures in Spanish America. The Spanish elites could not and did not demand full assimilation to Spanish culture, though certainly their language and culture dominated. English colonists eschewed (or at least pretended to eschew) mixing with indigenous peoples, and they established settler colonies with a more rigid racial hierarchy. Indians were savages outside the bounds of the nation. African slaves were part of an inferior race, destined for servitude, never citizens. As colonial leaders across the Americas began to imagine themselves as part of something distinct from the colonizing nations, they imagined these new nations according to racial orders they had inherited. Thus, for example, the U.S. Constitution in its original form made no provision for the citizenship or participation of indigenous people, while most nineteenth-century Latin American constitutions explicitly declared indigenous people to be equal citizens under the law (though that rarely translated to equal rights in the concrete).[21] In both cases, the culture and language of European migrants dominated, though attempts at assimilating indigenous inhabitants ultimately had greater destructive effects on local cultures in North America.

Only in the twentieth century did most European colonies in Africa, Asia, and the Pacific achieve independence. But by the beginning of the twenty-first century, the entire world was divided into nation-states with central governments and borders. This seemingly tidy division of the world, however, rarely constitutes a perfect match to ethnic, cultural, or religious identities in the real world. Absurdities abound: "Whatever your background, if you have a French identity card, you are French; if you have a Turkish identity card, you are Turkish even if you were born a Kurd."[22] Borders are imposed, while cultural boundaries remain porous; people migrate not as individuals but as cultural communities, and religious groups retain a presence in areas claimed by other religious groups. The Hutu and Tutsi ethnic groups (which speak the same language) are spread across the Democratic Republic of the Congo, Rwanda, Burundi, and other nations. The ancient communities of Assyrian and Chaldean Christians remain in Iraq, an ostensibly Muslim state. The Buddhist state of Myanmar (Burma) claims that ethnically Rohingya Muslims are immigrants from Bangladesh, but the assertion is demonstrably false. Hindi and Urdu, and Croatian and Serbian, respectively, are essentially the same language, though separated by borders between India and Pakistan and Croatia and Serbia and written in distinct alphabets. A monument assiduously marking the U.S.–Mexico border now lies entirely on the Mexican side of a border wall, next to a fenced-in no-man's-land officially called "Friendship Park." Yet, despite the absurdities, the modern idea of the nation-state as absolute has a strong cultural and structural hold on today's world.

Even as this world of nation-states developed through the early modern period, religious leaders generally acquiesced to it, in part because they had lost some of their influence; in part because religion served as a marker of national identity; and in part because governments protected the monopolies of state churches. The development of a more secular political order in the wake of the Enlightenment, however, did not always sit well with religious leaders. The eruption of the French Revolution—especially in its anticlerical and antireligious phase—troubled many Catholic leaders. Liberal governments, which supported (limited) voting rights and a free market economy, emerged in several Catholic states, including the newly independent states of Latin America and the emerging Kingdom of Italy. The latter displaced the previously liberal Pope Pius IX from his rule over the Papal States. He and his successors turned against liberal thought, describing democracy and political and religious liberties as religious errors. The antimodern bias in Catholicism effectively lasted until the Second Vatican Council in the 1960s. Even so, the problems of the modern age, among them the exploitation of workers and new waves of migration, did not wait for Catholic leaders to make their peace with modernity. By the 1890s, even the antimodernist pope, Leo XIII, realized he had to say something. What he wrote on the subject of workers and their rights launched a body of religious teaching that eventually treated migration extensively. It is now known as Catholic social teaching.

CATHOLIC SOCIAL TEACHING AND MIGRATION

Although Catholic social teaching eventually addressed migration directly, it first emerged as a body of Catholic doctrine in response to the industrial revolution. Starting in the eighteenth century in Great Britain, industrialization—characterized by the rise of the manufacturing of goods in factories and distribution of those goods by rail and steamship—accelerated across Europe, North America, and Japan, and into Latin America during the nineteenth century. In many places, factory labor created troublesome and even dangerous working conditions, including long hours, constant injuries, child labor, and low wages. Industrialization also spurred internal migration from rural to urban areas. Many governments, taken by the laissez-faire "liberalism" of the day, hesitated to intervene in any way. Religious leaders were caught off guard. The rural parish was the lifeblood and institutional center of the state churches of Europe, and "quite simply they were unable to move fast enough into the rapidly growing cities where their 'people' now resided; as a result they increasingly lost their control over the beliefs and behavior of European populations."[23] The popes and bishops in Europe also remained distracted by other controversies, including battles over secular political ideologies unleashed by the French Revolution, modernist ideas in theology, papal infallibility, and the slow loss of papal political control in Italy.

By 1891, however, Pope Leo XIII realized that the Church had to respond to the impoverishment and exploitation of workers, in part because Catholic workers were seeking support elsewhere, primarily in socialist trade unions. His *Rerum Novarum* used the medieval theology of Thomas Aquinas to steer between the extremes of totally unregulated capitalism and a socialism that favored government control of the entire economy. Leo defended private property, including the private ownership of factories, but he also thought that employers were morally bound to pay their workers a just wage and not whatever was negotiated between these unequal parties. He argued workers had the right to organize in unions, perhaps romanticizing the late medieval workers' guilds that had disappeared. The state should intervene when people are oppressed, but religion could be an even more effective tool to guide the wealthy and powerful to understand their duties to the poor who worked for them.[24] Leo XIII hardly mentioned migrants and migration in this first document in the tradition of Catholic social teaching, only pausing to note that if the poor shared in the ownership of property, they would not need or desire to leave their homeland for another country (*Rerum Novarum* 47). Of course, migrants would benefit from the recognition of the rights of workers articulated in *Rerum Novarum*.

Leo and his successors promoted ministerial outreach to migrants and occasionally lobbied on their behalf, but the first explicit teaching on migrants and migration in Catholic social teaching does not occur until 1952 with Pope Pius XII's *Exsul Familia Nazarethana*. In this apostolic constitution, Pius XII had on his mind Arab refugees recently displaced by the war for Israel's independence in 1948, but also the continuing crisis of migrants and refugees in Europe following the Second World War. For years after the end of the war, millions of people remained in refugee camps, including Eastern European slave laborers kidnapped to Germany during the war. In this document, Pius XII placed migrants in the heart of the Church, noting what church leaders had done for their material and spiritual well-being past and present. He worried about the separation of families in forced migrations and deportations. Finally, Pius lifted up as patron and example the family of Jesus, Mary, and Joseph, themselves displaced by King Herod's murderous political machinations (Matt 2:13–23):

122

> The émigré Holy Family of Nazareth, fleeing into Egypt, is the archetype of every refugee family. Jesus, Mary, and Joseph, living in exile in Egypt to escape the fury of an evil king, are, for all times and all places, the models and protectors of every migrant, alien, and refugee of whatever kind who, whether compelled by fear of persecution or by want, is forced to leave his native land, his beloved parents and relatives, his close friends, and to seek a foreign soil. (*Exsul Familia Nazarethana*, introduction)

This was more than a pious recommendation; it grounded the pope's later assertion that migrants and refugees, when their own country cannot provide, have a natural—that is, God-given—human right to migrate. This assertion shapes the entire body of Catholic social teaching regarding migration.[25]

Pope John XXIII took the emerging teaching about migration to its logical conclusion. A jolly former diplomat with a gift for the humorous remark, when asked by reporters how many people worked at the Vatican, he famously quipped, "About half." John nevertheless devoted himself to the concerns of his age in encyclical letters like *Pacem in Terris* (1963), where he addressed the growing dangers of the Cold War's nuclear standoff and the widening economic gap between wealthy and poor nations. In that letter, the first addressed not just to Catholics but to all people, he reiterated Pius XII's assertion of the human rights of refugees and migrants (in nos. 25 and 105–6). Now he rooted that assertion in the unity of the human race: "The fact that [a migrant] is a citizen of a particular State does not deprive him of membership in the human family, nor of citizenship in that universal society, the common, worldwide fellowship of [human beings]" (no. 25). Pope John lamented how economic inequality caused so many to leave their homes (no. 71), wanted foreign workers to receive the same rights as native-born workers (no. 71), and argued for a welcome from receiving countries followed by a gradual integration process (no. 69).[26]

By this time then, most of the basic principles of Catholic social teaching regarding migration were in place. People have the right to migrate if they are unable to flourish in their own land; receiving countries should offer hospitality and gradual integration; church and state should help to reunite families, not tear them apart; and immigrant workers should have the same rights as local workers. As the priest and migration scholar Enzo Marchetto notes, these rights remained a minor part of Church teaching, however, until the worldwide gathering of Catholic bishops at the Second Vatican Council. That Council, summoned by John XXIII to precipitate a reform or "update" (*aggiornamento*) in Catholic life, turned the Church's face toward the exterior world and its human needs:

> It is in the documents of the Second Vatican Council that the issue of social justice became the core of the Church's teaching. The usual themes of spiritual assistance, the administration of Sacraments and preaching in the immigrants' language as a safeguard against apostasy, and the duty of both rich and poorly populated countries toward accepting people from overpopulated areas became of secondary importance to the question of international justice.[27]

The Council's documents also pointed out that culture matters to human beings, and thus, migrants should not be forced to abandon theirs. The bishops argued that the many cultures of the world are a human good, that they enrich any nation where cultures coexist.[28]

After the Second Vatican Council, both the more liberal Pope Paul VI and the more conservative Pope John Paul II maintained that nationalism, economic progress, and an exaggerated concern for national security should not be used to justify the mistreatment of migrants. But Paul VI also admitted that migrants have responsibilities to gradually accommodate themselves to their new home. John Paul II rooted migrant rights in the God-given dignity of all human beings and in that solidarity—that is, care and responsibility for one another—that comes from our shared humanity, no matter our differences. People should not have to migrate, but when they do, receiving communities should offer them hospitality.[29]

Both John Paul II and his successor Benedict XVI pointed out that cooperation between nations was crucial to addressing both migration and border issues.[30] Consequently, in 2003, the Catholic bishops' conferences of Mexico and the United States together wrote a pastoral letter on migration, "Strangers No Longer: Together on the Journey of Hope." In this document, they recall that both their nations have received many migrants over the centuries of their existence and that their shared border demands cooperation, as well as recognition of the two countries' economic interdependence. They remember the biblical stories of migration noted in the previous chapter, and they summarize in five principles the cumulative contribution of Catholic social teaching on migration:

> 1) Persons have the right to find opportunities in their homeland....2) Persons have the right to migrate to support themselves and their families....3) Sovereign nations have the right to control their borders....4) Refugees and asylum seekers should be afforded protection....5) The human dignity and human rights of undocumented migrants should be respected.[31]

The bishops recognize the theological roots of these principles, including the protection of the common good, the God-given dignity of all human beings whatever their legal status, and the fact that the goods of the earth are meant for all people, not just some of them. They then lay out the pastoral challenges created by migration and their joint responsibility to address them. They end with public policy prescriptions and recommendations they hope the governments of their two nations will enact (they enacted few).

Catholic social teaching is a living tradition, still being developed as we speak. In 2013, an Argentinean archbishop with a history of pastoral work in his nation's slums, Jorge Bergoglio, became Pope Francis. While also pursuing an agenda of reform in the Vatican bureaucracy, or curia, the pope has asked Christians to go to the peripheries of the world and care for the marginalized. He speaks of God's special love for the poor, or what Catholic theologians call "the preferential option for the poor." Francis calls for a "culture of encounter" where people's differences bear fruit in their deep engagement with one another. He highlights mercy as the heart of the Christian gospel, a mercy extended to all, including those who often feel they have little place in the Church, such as LGBT people, victims of human trafficking, and the divorced and remarried.[32]

Not surprisingly, Pope Francis has returned to the early Christian idea that hospitality to migrants, including to those without legal papers, is a central demand of the Christian gospel: "Migrants present to me a particular challenge, because I am pastor of a Church without borders, a Church which feels itself the mother of all. Therefore, I exhort all countries to a generous openness, one which remains capable of creating new cultural syntheses, instead of fearing the destruction of national identity" (*Evangelli Gaudium* 210).[33]

Since Francis became pope, several nations—Hungary, Poland, Russia, the Philippines, Brazil, Italy, the United States, and the United Kingdom—elected or reelected populist leaders with nationalist agendas. They prioritized not only the unapologetic supremacy of their own nation or culture, some to the point of extolling racial or ethnic purity and others withdrawing from international agreements and organizations, but also strong efforts to reduce the immigration of outsiders drastically. They especially punished immigrants without legal papers. In many ways, the pope's teaching on migration is simply a new synthesis of previous teaching, with a few innovations like the emphasis on a "culture of encounter." But in the context of the new nationalism, he sounds to some like a revolutionary. His contributions, along with the whole body of Catholic social teaching on migration, have influenced contemporary theological and ethical scholarship on migration, even that of Christian scholars who are not Catholic. We turn now to that scholarship.

Chapter Eight

MIGRATION IN CHRISTIAN ETHICS

When I was researching at a multicultural Catholic parish in the Midwest, a young immigrant from Mexico told me the story of how one day his car broke down on a deserted rural road. Undocumented immigrants in those days often drove without licenses or registration (as they still do in some states where they are legally unable to obtain them), and to avoid any legal entanglements that might end in deportation, they would take rural roads less frequented by police officers. I am not sure if this was how it started for this young man, but he found himself on the side of the road in need of help. This was in the days before many people had cell phones. In his telling, the story sounded much like that of the Good Samaritan (Luke 10:25–37): several automobiles with fellow Mexican immigrants at the wheel drove right by, until a white family stopped and then drove him to a mechanic in town. He emphasized to me, a white man, that several people from his own community would not help, but this one, kind white family, with whom he had no connection, did stop to come to the aid of a stranger.

This story reminds me of the Christian morality classes that I took in Catholic high school. We were always struggling with case studies like this one, moral dilemmas that helped us think through our ethical responsibilities to other people. Some of the case studies were classics — the old dilemmas, for example, about insufficient food for persons in a lifeboat, or whether it is moral to sacrifice individuals to save a greater number of people. I remember that my teacher, a former seminarian and

127

pacifist, particularly liked to give us dilemmas that questioned whether violence was ever ethical. We were told these discussions were what was called moral theology, though scholars today more often refer to the religious study of such questions as Christian ethics.

I had the impression, intended or not, that studying ethics was mainly about having an answer for these sticky moral dilemmas. If I had thought at all about the ethics of migration at that time, I probably would have assumed it was exactly to address a situation described by that young man. What should a person do when confronted by an immigrant stranger in need? While this is a very important question, it does not come close to helping us discover our *communal* responsibilities toward migrants and migration as a neighborhood, a city, a faith community, or even as an entire nation-state. It gives us no guidance toward political reforms that might help people. It does not help us rethink immigration in the face of those myriad community or cultural narratives presented several chapters ago.

Clearly this view of ethics is shaped by the individualism of Western life over the last few centuries. We see each person as an autonomous individual, responsible mainly just for themselves. Faith becomes privatized, a matter of an individual's personal relationship with God. Ethics becomes a question of how as individuals we should behave when we encounter other individuals. Communities and nations— even families—are seen as voluntary gatherings of individuals, and so the emphasis stays on how each individual chooses to behave toward discrete others. We do not really think about the way our behavior impacts larger systems, or the cultures of which we are a part. All that feels far away, beyond our influence, even though, objectively, it is the product of the decisions we make when taken together.

At the same time, as the early sociologist Max Weber observed, our societies have become compartmentalized, where each area of life—work, family, religion, government, commerce—has its own sphere of influence and its own goals and ideals, unrelated to other areas.[1] Immigration law and policy then lie securely in the "compartment" of government and law. Faith has little to do with it, even if the tenets and practices of Christianity have definite implications about what is just or unjust in that area of life. For this reason, most immigration policy decisions are shaped not by faith or even secular ethical thinking but by implicit political theories, especially what is termed "political realism." Political realists accept that immigrants have no intrinsic rights except when nation-states generously grant them, and how generously they do should depend on a careful cost-benefit analysis.[2]

Christian ethics is not blameless in this ethical abandonment of the public square. For centuries, the manuals of moral theology or Christian ethics were full of case studies and dilemmas focused on individual behavior. Finally, as noted in the final section of the previous chapter, something happened at the end of the nineteenth century and the beginning of the twentieth century. As the industrial revolution introduced widespread difficult working conditions and created a new class of urban poor in Europe, it became impossible for Christian leaders to attend only to questions of charity, ministry, or individual responsibility for the neighbor. Protestant theologians began to speak of the social gospel, that is, the demands for a more just and equitable society embedded in the preaching of Jesus and the Old Testament prophets. At the same time, Roman Catholic pastoral leaders began to enlist students and workers in a process of reflection on the social problems wrought by the industrial revolution, and various bishops and popes began to enunciate principles and teaching to guide Catholics longing for a more just society. Those principles and teaching became known as Catholic social teaching or doctrine, described in some detail in the previous chapter.

Of course, the new Christian social ethics that emerged from this era was not entirely new. Protestant ethicists continued to rely on biblical theology as an ethical foundation, and Catholics continued to reflect on principles of justice intuited by medieval theologians as part of natural law, that is, the God-given social order that a perceptive observer could detect. During the Middle Ages in Europe, the Dominican friar and theologian Thomas Aquinas had written about the responsibilities of Christian rulers to guide their subjects toward the common good. Two centuries later, as the Protestant Reformation unfolded around him, Martin Luther carefully reflected on what a Christian society ought to look like in light of both biblical demands for justice and the imperfections of a sinful society. Christian social ethics in the twentieth century worked from these foundations to an analysis of the social problems of modern life and to the specific rights and responsibilities of modern people in the midst of these social problems.

THEOLOGICAL NARRATIVES AND MIGRATION

To return to the Midwestern town where I conducted research in the early 2000s, the new social ethics would be less interested in a moral dilemma that unfolded with a car broken down on a rural road and more interested in the conditions that led a man to stick to deserted roads lest he be deported and separated from his U.S.-born children. Local manufacturing had created a demand for factory labor that could not be met by the aging population of the town, and Mexican immigrants had answered the call, though many had no means of obtaining legal status as they did, and companies had almost no means or motivation to assist them. In such a situation, where the economic common good of the town depended on the factories, what responsibilities—if any—did those born there have toward these newcomers? One Anglo parishioner suggested that, under such circumstances, white Catholics had a duty to welcome the newcomers to their parish without making any demands for linguistic and cultural assimilation. Another saw the newcomers as taking advantage of the few services available to them (emergency medical care, public schools) and thought that whites in town had no responsibility toward them.

Who was right? Christian social ethics attempts to answer such a question not simply as a practical matter but rooted in a clear set of principles that make sense within a Christian worldview. For all Christians, these principles and that worldview have their clearest roots in the teachings of Jesus and the Hebrew prophets as recorded in the Bible. Protestant ethics generally begins there, especially Evangelical Protestant ethics, though most Protestant ethicists also build on the previous reflections of other ethicists and theologians. Contemporary Catholic ethicists do the same, but they tend to add Catholic social teaching as a kind of second foundation for ethical reflection on society and its problems. In our day and age, almost all Christian theologians operate ecumenically—they include not only their coreligionists in their reflections but also scholars from other Christian traditions. Not all Christian ethicists, of course, come to the same conclusions. It is worth noting, however, that few Christian ethicists argue for a social ethics that allows the citizens of a nation to claim exclusive privileges or that sees the dramatic restriction of immigration as an ethical response. However, let us turn to the work of that group of ethical thinkers first.

130

OBEDIENCE TO THE STATE AND PRIORITY TO ITS CITIZENS

Christian ethical thinkers who believe that there should be limits to the hospitality extended to immigrants generally root their work in the thinking of St. Augustine, a fifth-century North African bishop, perhaps the most influential theologian of Western Christianity. Augustine was confronted with the sacking of Rome's imperial capital by the German tribes in 410. Not a few pagan thinkers blamed Christianity for the cataclysm, arguing that the empire was receiving its just rewards for abandoning the traditional gods. Augustine's defense of Christianity is known by its short title, *The City of God*, but it is largely an argument that God's favor kept the empire relatively intact. And a good part of Augustine's argument is that God's perfect "city" with its devoted "citizens," who love God above all, must coexist both in the world and in the Church with a human, or earthly, "city" damaged by sin and occupied by those given over to selfishness.

In short, while the reign of God is still not complete, human beings must work within the institutions and structures of the earthly city. "For Augustine, the politics of an instance of the earthly city is about negotiating what is necessary for a tolerable earthly peace to exist, within which the Gospel can be preached and which the heavenly city makes use of for a time."[3] To paraphrase, since no one can definitively sort out the good and the bad in a society, Christians should make a practical peace with the authorities, in particular, so they will be allowed to share the Christian message. Martin Luther, writing at the dawn of the era of the nation-state in the early 1500s, built on this foundation to argue that sin made it impossible for human beings to conform fully to the ideals and demands of God's kingdom or reign. Until Jesus's return and the culmination of everything, Christians had to obey both God's Word and the demands of the earthly kingdom as established by God, an argument he repeated to defend the violent suppression of the Peasants' Revolt of 1524 and 1525.[4]

The logic of the two cities and the two kingdoms means Christians, despite their commitment to compassionate love and the dignity of all, need not feel ambivalent about limiting migration, defending borders, or supporting state action against unauthorized immigration and immigrants. Christians are obligated to support the state in its divine mission to keep order in the world, which includes the establishment of borders, in part so that the Church can go about its spiritual mission of preaching Christ, protected by that order.[5] The incarnation itself (God becoming human in Jesus) argues for the importance of respecting particular human communities—family, city, nation.

This leads us to another teaching of St. Augustine, that of the *ordo amoris*, the order of love. Christians must love everyone, but they should prioritize those whom God has put immediately in their path. "Because it was God's will to give us the identities we experience as given, our initial loyalty is to the neighbors God has made closest to us."[6] British ethicist Esther Reed perhaps goes the furthest in identifying what the famous Protestant theologian Karl Barth called our "near neighbors" (versus our far neighbors to whom we may owe less) with our cocitizens.[7] The Oxford theologian Nigel Biggar similarly argues that, because human beings are culturally and geographically embedded creatures, people have the right to control borders and to prioritize the needs of citizens, what he calls a "morally limited right to autonomy over material and social assets":

> Borders exist primarily to define the territory within which a people is free to develop its own way of life as best it can. Unrestricted mobility would permit uncontrolled immigration that would naturally be experienced by natives as an invasion. Successful, peaceful immigration needs to be negotiated: immigrants must demonstrate a willingness to respect the ways of their native hosts and to a certain extent abide by them; natives must be given time to accommodate new residents and their foreignness.[8]

According to these thinkers, there is nothing wrong with restricting immigration or deporting unauthorized immigrants if it is to ensure that there is order for one's own people.

Still, it is worth noting that many of the Christian ethicists who take this position still argue for a process by which such unauthorized or undocumented immigrants could become citizens; there is virtually no Christian ethicist who would echo the rhetoric of mass deportations or severe restriction of immigration espoused by the immigrant threat narratives we explored in chapter 3. Nigel Biggar, for example, contends that a truly Christian ethic of the nation cannot tolerate completely closed borders or the scapegoating of other nations to whip up nationalist loyalty.[9] Other ethicists of this ilk point to particular duties toward refugees, though they are less likely to critique the limitations of today's legal definition of refugees. Again, virtually no ethicist today would argue that there is no Christian duty toward refugees at all, as is espoused in today's nationalist populism.[10] Nevertheless, these ethicists come under criticism by other ethicists and theologians; their spirited defense of prioritizing one's own cocitizens seems to some to contradict one's Christian duty toward the neighbor. Evangelical ethicist Justin Ashworth, for example, suggests that the defense of strong borders ignores the way militarized borders create conditions for harm, whether that harm be manhandling by Border Patrol agents, vigilante threats, sexual assault by criminal organizations, or death while crossing inhospitable deserts. He believes that Christians' first loyalty must be to the Church, a people that transcends borders and exists everywhere, and a people in solidarity with all who suffer as Christ did.[11]

A BIBLICAL AND PROPHETIC ETHIC

While some Christian ethicists prioritize the state's right to restrict immigration and Christians' responsibility to obey the state, most do not. "Christian migration ethics has generally answered the question of responsibility to noncitizens by affirming the full humanity and dignity of migrants: migrants are humans made in the image of God."[12] This generally leads to an emphasis on human rights that at times transcends the sovereignty rights of the nation-state. Thus, for most Protestant and Catholic ethicists, "the cultivation of a distinct national life must be subordinated to the concern for an international order of justice and freedom."[13] The nation-state's prioritizing of its own citizens must not be so absolute that it fails basic Christian tests of caring for the weak or the marginal. Special concern for one's fellow citizens does not relieve anyone of basic Christian responsibility to ease suffering when they can or to care for the wounded in our midst, including when those wounded are refugees or migrants from afar.

Moreover, for many Protestant ethicists, the Augustinian-Lutheran conception of the two cities or kingdoms means that the nation-state remains a *provisional* instrument of God's order and justice. Any peace or justice on the sinful earth will necessarily be incomplete, a mere echo of the peace and justice that will descend on earth at the advent of God's reign.[14] This relativizes the kind of obedience any Christian owes to the state, and it undermines any ethical argument that absolutizes the distinction between an immigrant who comes lawfully and one who arrives unauthorized.

Indeed, for most Protestant ethicists, migration ethics begins not with a theology of the state but with the biblical witness recounted in chapter 6. As the Baptist ethicist Miguel de la Torre notes, "Even a casual reading of the Scriptures reveals the prominence of the alien—the stranger within our midst—throughout our biblical narrative. The people of God are constantly reminded to welcome and love the stranger for they too were once aliens in a strange land."[15] De la Torre counts thirty-eight injunctions in the Torah, or Pentateuch, to this effect, and he argues that they are rooted first in the specific experience of Israel being enslaved in a foreign land. To oppress strangers would be a monumental hypocrisy. Second, he argues that immigrant hospitality is rooted in God's special love for the poor and marginalized, a theme that emerges in the Torah or covenantal law but finds deeper expression in the work of the Old Testament prophets who take Israelites to task for oppressing the poor and the stranger. "To be an alien is to live without the societal and familial structures that can provide protection...radically vulnerable to those already living in a place."[16] Receiving communities have a responsibility not only to not take advantage of that vulnerability, but to provide hospitality in light of it. After all, Jesus, to whom Christians are bonded in their baptism, was a vulnerable "divine alien" in this world, and he lived his life in solidarity with the vulnerable as a result.

Finally, de la Torre suggests that hospitality to the stranger is rooted in a notion of the common good embedded in Israel's covenant with God. Part of the reason there are definitive biblical rules about welcoming the stranger, caring for the widow and the orphan, and making sure workers are not abused is that God made a covenant of love not only with elites or citizens but with everyone who lives on the land. Through the later prophets—the second prophet who speaks in the Book of Isaiah, the satirical Jonah, Malachi, and Zechariah—that covenantal concern is revealed to be for all human beings, a theme that the New Testament takes up as well. The message of Jesus was meant to cross boundaries and invite in everyone. The concomitant responsibility for all in need comes through most clearly in the parable of the Good Samaritan (Luke 10:25–37), where the Samaritan foreigner has the proper sense of responsibility for his wounded Judean neighbor, even when Judean leaders walk right by and ignore the one in need.

CATHOLIC SOCIAL TEACHING AND THE ETHICS OF MIGRATION

If the Protestant social ethics of migration usually begins with biblical foundations, a Roman Catholic social ethics of migration tends to proceed by echoing, building on, or critically assessing Catholic social teaching, that body of principles and directives discussed at the end of chapter 7 on migration in Christian history. Catholic social teaching has significant roots in Scripture, especially in the theological idea that humanity was created as *imago Dei*, that is, in God's image and likeness (Gen 1:26–27). One important ethical consequence of this idea is that human beings have an innate God-given dignity that must be respected. In other words, no government, corporation, or other institution should be permitted to treat a human person as if they were a nonperson, a means to an end, or "collateral damage" in some greater project. This is why Catholic social ethics finds both unfettered laissez-faire capitalism and state-controlled communism unacceptable as political economies—they both easily sacrifice particular human beings in the service of larger society-wide projects, projects that often amount to power or wealth for the few. This is also why Catholic social ethicists generally criticize governments for immigration regimens that make insufficient space for refugees or justify the detention or mistreatment of unauthorized immigrants simply because they are on the wrong side of the law.

Catholic social teaching is generally expressed in abstract teachings, a not surprising development considering they are meant to apply to the entire world with its wildly different contexts and events. However, since the Second Vatican Council's turn toward the concerns of the world, Catholic social ethics has often embraced these principles with attentiveness to the actual crises and concerns of the contexts in which people live and work. A good example is the work of Jesuit ethicist William O'Neill on migration. O'Neill has not only taught at Jesuit schools of theology in the United States and Kenya but also served refugees displaced by war and famine in camps run by Jesuit Refugee Services in Africa. Drawing on this experience, he freely but sadly acknowledges that, for many people, "refugees are increasingly perceived, not as victims but as perpetrators of insecurity."[17]

O'Neill wants to bring to bear the principles of Catholic social teaching on this resistance rooted in fear of the other. But he knows that our international system of nation-states and citizenship, while rooted in the political liberalism of the Enlightenment, primarily bestows rights on citizens. The rights of migrants enumerated by Catholic social teaching and based on their common humanity—the right to migrate, to find safety in a new land, for families not to be separated, to hospitality—have little justification in a global political system where individual rights are bestowed and protected by the state for its own people. "Our very *right to have rights* typically depends on citizenship in a particular state."[18] Noncitizens, foreigners, and even more so unauthorized immigrants are theoretically owed only the duty of forbearance, that is, they are not to be subjected to harm or injury. This is why, for example, immigration courts do not grant immigrants most of the usual rights associated with citizens. They do not have the right to counsel, due process, and a speedy trial; protection from detention without charge; or protection from unreasonable search and seizure. This leads to odd outcomes in immigration court or detention, such as when very young children are asked to represent themselves in court or when people's Bibles or Qur'ans are confiscated.

According to the modern Western legal regime, citizens do not owe migrants and refugees anything. Hospitality to them is an act of charity or kindness, never a duty. And indeed, many North Americans view hospitality to immigrants and refugees as a nice thing to do, but a habit that can be jettisoned should other more pressing citizen concerns present themselves. Thus, for example, if people see migrants as a national security risk or stealing jobs, or if there are simply too many, it is perfectly fine to not "do the nice thing" and to build walls, shut down the border, or reduce the refugee quota to nearly zero (as done during the Trump administration). O'Neill argues, however, that this logic is fundamentally not Christian. It conflicts with the biblical injunction to love one's neighbor as oneself, which both the Hebrew prophets and Jesus of Nazareth argue includes caring for the stranger as if that person were part of one's own community. In the biblical parable of the Good Samaritan (Luke 10:25–37), the self-justifying scribe asks, "Who is my neighbor?" Jesus answers with a story in which only a stranger and foreigner recognizes the duty to care for an injured man; the man's own countrymen pass him by. In Catholic social teaching, all persons are made in God's image and are part of the human community, the stranger as much as one's family and friends. Moreover, in God's plan, the goods of the earth are meant for everyone, not just one nation. Thus, care for the stranger is a moral duty rather than an optional act of charity.

As in the Good Samaritan story, that duty intensifies when the stranger is suffering and in immediate need. O'Neill argues that the "preferential option for the poor" in Catholic social teaching echoes this truth, that the more vulnerable and marginalized a person is, the greater the responsibility. This creates what he calls "the moral priority of relative need."[19] "Our very moral entitlement to equal respect or consideration justifies preferential treatment for those whose basic rights are most imperiled."[20] When children come to the southern border fleeing gang violence in the Northern Triangle of Central America, for example, O'Neill would argue that their basic right to life, health, and safety trumps others' rights to freedom from worry about the tax burden or demographic changes that may occur as a result of taking them in. You cannot send a child back to a violent situation to protect your own peace of mind. In parallel, in terms of public policy, for an affluent country such as the United States or Canada to reduce the number of refugees to nearly zero is morally wrong.

One of the foremost North American Catholic ethicists working on migration today is Kristin Heyer, who teaches at Boston College. Like O'Neill, Heyer begins with Catholic social teaching and the dignity of the human person it implies. She focuses attention on the way various societal factors dehumanize immigrants, beginning with the economy, noting that "reductive conceptualizations of immigrants are dehumanizing whether they cast persons as social burdens or economically beneficial."[21] The contemporary economic order demonstrates a tendency to "reduce laborers to 'factors of production' [fostering] dehumanizing conditions that generate economic refugees in the first place, and then exploit undocumented workers who remain precariously vulnerable once hired."[22] She points to the example of Mexican agricultural laborers whose livelihood was decimated by free trade policies beginning in the 1990s. There was no provision in U.S. law to accommodate the resulting millions who sought work in the United States when they could not find it in Mexican cities. Thus, in contrast to the threat or even the rule of law cultural narrative, which both depict unauthorized immigrants from Mexico and Central America as illicitly motivated schemers who pose a threat, these women and men were more accurately people cast from their customary living and seeking a way to make ends meet.[23]

Heyer also points out how post-9/11 national security concerns have often turned immigrants into scapegoats rather than people. Even before the 2001 attacks, various political and media voices celebrated "social construals of national identity over and against the outsider,"[24] not infrequently identifying U.S. citizenship with European ancestry and defining "outsider" as those with darker skin. This implied racial calculus then justifies the deaths of unauthorized migrants crossing in the desert, who evade stepped-up border enforcement policies in safer areas; many Americans treat their suffering and death as an acceptable cost for deterrence. Commonplace sexual assault at the border is similarly disregarded. Such disregard only becomes possible, Heyer argues, when receiving communities minimize the humanity of such immigrants, seeing them not as people having to make courageous choices in a world of limits, but simply as lawbreakers and irritants.[25]

Heyer associates these negative views of immigrants—as commodities, scapegoats, or irritants—with the Christian notion of *sin*, specifically what ethicists call *social sin*. While many Christians today think of sin as the personal breaking of laws or rules instituted by God (perhaps disproportionately associated with sexual misbehavior), biblical authors like St. Paul tended to see sin more as a condition inherent to human life and culture that distances us from God and propels us toward lives of self-destruction and harm toward others. The Catholic moral tradition has historically focused more attention on personal sin, thus shortchanging the influence larger social forces have on us and how we ourselves contribute to those larger forces. Our earlier discussion of the cultural narratives that mislead us demonstrate the destructive power of these social forces.

Heyer follows theologian Gregory Baum's account of social sin, describing it as occurring via (1) institutions that embody injustice and dehumanizing trends; (2) cultural narratives and ideologies that legitimize injustice and harm to others; (3) the blindness or false consciousness that institutions or ideologies may engender in us, including silent complicity; and (4) decisions made by communities and organizations that lead to more injustice and harm.[26] To make the model concrete, we can consider the "surge" of Central American families and unaccompanied children who began to appear at the U.S.–Mexico border in 2014 requesting asylum. Most of these families came fleeing gang threats and extortion in Honduras, Guatemala, and El Salvador, most often from two international gangs, MS-13 and Calle-18. The institutionalized injustice becomes visible when we see that these gangs originated in the United States, and they ended up in Central America primarily because (1) U.S. states targeted gang members for arrest and prosecution, often of minor drug crimes, and (2) the federal government then deported convicted gang members not born in the United States, including those who were legal residents. U.S. government institutions simply pushed the problem off on someone else.

These policies, of course, depended on cultural narratives that legitimated them. Gang members were depicted by political leaders and in the media as violent predators, even when they were more likely to be teens and young adults with no prospects. The families and children who arrived starting in 2014 were often described in the media as a problem overwhelming the system, not as people with stories of great suffering back home. The combination of these policies, narratives, and ideologies created a kind of blindness. Americans did not understand why this was happening, had little interest in finding out, and often accepted untruths without serious examination, assuming, for example, that the gangs had their origins in Central America. The public decided to accept the Obama administration's characterization of this as a problem of institutions overwhelmed, and the administration instituted expedited proceedings for minors to resolve the overload. In the end, children from other countries found they had only three weeks to procure an attorney, something most had no idea how to do without assistance from nonprofit organizations.[27]

This may be how social sin works in the concrete, but who then is culpable or responsible for such collective problems? Heyer is unwilling to let us all off the hook. She acknowledges that very often we do not understand what is happening because we willfully neglect finding out. Those who work in media prioritize drama or good relationships with sources over dissemination of the truth, and those of us who consume media fail to ask deeper questions or fact-check using other sources. We vote for political leaders who insist that harsh measures will spare us higher crime rates, without considering whether this is true or morally justifiable. Much complicity, she argues, is simply silence. During the 2016 election, then-candidate Trump sought the support of white nationalists and other hard-liners with increasingly insulting comments, not only about undocumented immigrants, but about Mexican and other Latin American immigrants in general. Though most of the insulted were Catholics, very few Catholic bishops and even fewer priests objected in any public way. Heyer's model suggests that by doing so they were complicit and guilty of sin.

According to Heyer, however, the answer is not to simply condemn anyone's participation in harm done to migrants but to get those who are complicit to change their minds and to change their behavior. The best route to such change—often in religion described as *conversion*—is actual encounters with immigrants and their stories and to do so as members of communities, churches, and other institutions. I teach graduate and undergraduate courses on migration, and these courses always have an "engaged learning" component that requires students to meet and listen to immigrants. Some accompany me across the southern border to a migrant shelter in Tijuana, Baja California, Mexico, to hear the stories of both refugees seeking asylum in the United States and deportees who have been forcibly separated from their families in the United States. Once students hear these stories and encounter these men, women, and children as people, they cannot unhear them. They often think, behave, and vote differently in regard to immigration policies. This is even more the case when they realize how immigration policies impact children and families.

MIGRATION, FAMILY, AND SOCIAL ETHICS

In January 2020, Sony Pictures Television broadcasted a remake of the 1990s television show *Party of Five* on the Freeform channel. But this time it treated not a family of five children who lost their parents to a car accident, but a family of five children whose parents are deported back to Mexico. In one poignant scene early on in the series, the preteen daughter, Valentina, makes an impassioned plea for mercy in immigration court, noting how she needs her parents. The judge nevertheless orders her parents deported, noting that the law does not allow relief from parental deportation except for in the most exceptional and dire of circumstances. While the series takes some creative liberties with the immigration experience, on this particular point it is utterly accurate. The situation holds even for single-parent families: "Undocumented single parents who have worked in the United States for a decade or longer are regularly deported because they can rarely meet this criterion."[28] In fact, thousands of children remain in foster care because a parent or both parents have been detained or deported.[29]

In earlier chapters of this work, we learned that migration decisions are often made at the family level rather than the individual level and that family reunification remains a powerful motivating narrative for immigrants. We heard that Catholic social teaching argues for the integrity of family life, in short, that families should not be separated by deportation. But to acknowledge these things is only to begin to consider the ethical questions that arise when we examine migration and family together. Despite North Americans' attachment to the notion of human persons as autonomous individuals, in truth we are built by and for relationships with others. Family in its many forms remains a foundational relationship for almost everyone, even when a harmfully dysfunctional family serves as a kind of obstacle to overcome. At their best, our families are schools of love who form people in the skills and character to be a force for good in society.[30]

If all this is true, that we are truly relational at heart, then immigration policies should look different. Governments should examine the numerical limits that lengthen waiting lists for family reunification for years and years. Needed parental caregiving should figure into the calculus of deportation, and not only in "exceptional" (usually life-threatening) cases. No state should make a parent choose, as at least one woman I know had to, between being with her spouse or with her children. Our deep need and hunger for connections should confront those elements of any threat narrative that make motherhood and childbearing into a menace (such as in the rhetoric of "anchor babies").[31] At the same time, this desire to safeguard the family should not ignore more complex and ambiguous aspects of family life. The demands of low-wage service work make little space for family life, yet these seldom make us question the ethics of the economy. Affluent families often hire immigrant women to care for their children so that both parents may pursue their careers, even though at least some of those women have children of their own back at home. On the one hand, this creates opportunities for those children through remittances—many young people from poorer families have become professionals in this way—but the practice can also reinforce the way in which child-rearing is seen almost exclusively as women's work.[32]

It would be less than honest not to admit that not only deportation but migration itself separates families at times, creating strange and lamentable situations. A lack of status makes this worse. Thus, an immigrant couple could not marry because a separated spouse back in Mexico refused to grant a divorce, and yet the undocumented husband could not return to Mexico to resolve the situation. A mother wept over the absence of her adult son and could not procure a visa to visit him, though the situation was resolved when he was able to regularize his situation, settle down, and start a family. A scientist who is the product of China's one-child policy worries about her parents as they grow older, even though they encouraged her to migrate. While Catholic social teaching argues that people have the right to migrate when their families cannot flourish at home, those same families surely debate the cost and benefits to their family. The very ways people conceive of family life, as ethicists like Kristin Heyer and Tisha Rajendra remind us, shape how immigrants and citizens see their responsibilities to migrant families.[33] An overly individualist conception of family usually implies that children have few responsibilities toward their parents, and this may allow for immigrant children to neglect parents left behind in sending communities. Citizens may see low-wage workers like servants whose families remain invisible. Employers may feel free to keep wages low because family and work remain compartmentalized from one another.

JUSTICE, RIGHTS, AND RELATIONSHIPS

The influence of these conceptions of family points to an important point by ethicist Tisha Rajendra of Loyola University Chicago. Justice consists not only in the protection of the rights of migrants but also in respect for the responsibilities created by our relationships. The child of immigrants from Sri Lanka, she is particularly interested in the relationship between citizens and migrants in the United States. The heart of her argument is that immigrants are not merely strangers to citizens.[34] Strangers, of course, have rights and are entitled to be treated respectfully, not harmed, and deserve aid if they are in danger or in particular need.[35] But migrants usually come from countries with a historical relationship to their new homeland. It is not an accident or a historical curiosity that people often migrate to nations that formerly colonized them (or vice versa)—Filipinos to the United States, Ukrainians to Russia (and the reverse), and Koreans to Japan. In a different way, for example, Mexicans cannot be seen simply as strangers in the United States, given the long sharing of a land border; an ill-begotten war that ended in the U.S. invasion of Mexico and compulsory surrender of territory; a significant trade relationship; and decades of people crossing back and forth.

Taking such a perspective brings us beyond viewing immigrants only through the lens of legal status, as in the rule of law narrative, and beyond determining responsibilities based on status. Regardless of status, as Rajendra notes, unauthorized immigrants and citizens do exist in relationship to one another, though often the latter have more trouble seeing that.[36] The truth of this has emerged in many conversations I have had with undocumented immigrants over the years. They point out how they contribute to the economy and that the vast majority pay taxes. Yet, that labor goes largely unappreciated, remunerated badly, mostly without benefits such as sick pay or health coverage, and accompanied by fear of deportation. Unauthorized immigrants see a certain hypocrisy in all of this. Americans depend on them to do this work, often work that many citizens will not do, but citizens refuse to acknowledge the contribution that work makes to the economy and society. Some industries, in fact, such as agricultural field work or construction, rely on unauthorized labor in dramatic ways. According to the U.S. Department of Agriculture, half of all farmworkers are undocumented.[37] Even so, and even given significant increases in the number of guest workers in recent years, growers routinely say they cannot find enough laborers for their harvests.[38]

Acknowledged or not, the contribution made by unauthorized immigrants creates a relationship between them and the citizens they serve. The rest of us, Rajendra argues, owe them something in return, especially given their low pay and bad working conditions. Nevertheless, the most politically liberal immigration reform proposals speak not of responsibilities but of "amnesty," that is, a generous forgiveness of their debt to society incurred by remaining in the country without status. Rajendra implies that legal status and a path to citizenship would be the least of it. Pay and working conditions must reflect the contribution they make, not simply be minimally compliant with law or respectful of basic human rights. We must be honest about the way in which unauthorized immigrants support not only the lifestyle of the affluent by serving as domestic workers or caregivers but the lifestyle of all of us who eat the food that they disproportionately harvest at considerable expense to their bodies.[39]

Rajendra's paradigm could be adjusted to examine internal migration as well, or the plight of refugees. We saw how millions of African Americans moved from the rural South to northern cities across the twentieth century. They found some welcome and success but also hostility and flight on the part of the whites they encountered. These whites may have considered Southern Blacks invaders or strangers, but they were neither. Euro-Americans and African Americans shared North America for four hundred years, including a slave-based economy where one race owned the other. Continuing afterward, institutionalized racial discrimination and bouts of white racial violence impeded African American economic progress and full citizenship, especially but not exclusively in the South. Like undocumented immigrants, many African Americans work at poorly remunerated jobs that nevertheless keep society going. Such a history and continuing arrangements imply responsibilities, perhaps chiefly a commitment on the part of whites to participate in the dismantling of racist institutions, a point not infrequently made during the demonstrations in response to the killing of unarmed Black people. It is also worth noting that refugees are also not strangers, perhaps the clearest case being recent refugee families from Central America, who left their homes fleeing the gangs that were quite literally deported from the United States to Central American cities. What do U.S. citizens owe them?

FROM ETHICS TO THEOLOGY

In this chapter, we have examined the contribution of Christian social ethics to understanding and living with migration. Social ethics offers one of the most common Christian narratives about migration, a narrative of rights and responsibilities, and that narrative often guides Christian leaders in proposing public policy and reform of immigration law in the United States as well as in other Western host nations. We saw how Scripture and Catholic social teaching have served as foundations for that narrative. Both tend to emphasize the needs and rights of migrants and encourage hospitality, and therefore, most social ethicists focus their reflections on those rights and on the responsibilities of citizens toward migrants. Only a small group argue for greater restriction of migration or limitation of migrants' rights. Questions surrounding migrant families have been a part of the social ethics narrative as well.

In fact, there is much more we could say about ethics and migration. Christianity has still more to say, however, that does not clearly fall under the category of ethics, that is, does not primarily tell a story about how human beings and their society should *behave* vis-à-vis immigrants and refugees. Some Christian scholars instead focus on what migration has to say about who we are as human beings, about who God is, and about what migration means in a world of sin and grace. We turn next to migration within theology.

Chapter Nine

MIGRATION IN THEOLOGY

On several different occasions now, I have done what I described in the very beginning of this book, that is, accompanied university students—graduate and undergraduate—on a trip to the U.S.–Mexico border. In the first chapter, I shared how evening conversations with refugees, migrants, and deportees have a way of focusing students' attention on the complexity of migration and the invisible suffering that many migrants and deportees endure. But my students also find another part of the trip interesting: our visit to the border fence. On the last trip, we traveled more or less straight to the very western edge of the border on the Mexican side, where the border meets the Pacific Ocean. That meeting takes place in Playas de Tijuana, an oceanfront *delegación*, or borough, that extends down the coast of the city of Tijuana. The northern corner of it next to the border includes a bullring, a bilingual stone border marker more than a century old, a small migrant shelter next to the beach, some exercise equipment, the beach itself, and countless restaurants where one can eat Baja-style fish tacos. There is also an enormous border fence that goes right out into the ocean.

Students whose notions of Mexico center on its poverty relative to the United States are initially surprised or perhaps delighted to find a beautiful tourist zone surrounded by expensive condominium buildings. But the Mexican side of the fence also serves as a kind of giant canvas for artists, professional and informal. Mexicans and Americans interpret migration between the two countries there. Over the waves on the fence sits the Playas de Tijuana Mural Project, a U.S.-based project featuring large, digitized images of several people who arrived in the United States from Mexico as children (and one deported U.S. veteran).[1] Some of the rest of the canvas is supervised by the Mexican artist Enrique Chiu as a *mural de la hermandad*, a mural of brotherhood or sisterhood.[2] There are bright colors, multitudinous hearts, butterflies (a favorite symbol of migration as rebirth), Scripture and literary quotes, declarations of love, traditional graffiti, and commentary both verbal and visual. *Somos todos migrantes*, says one section: We are all migrants. *No hay fronteras*, says another: There are no borders. There is a whole section of fence slats with the names of U.S. military veterans who were deported to Mexico, some deceased. Some of the texts are in Spanish, some in English.

When on different trips — my students have seen various iterations of this — they are struck by the juxtaposition of suffering and hope. The giant canvas on the Mexican side provides a stunning contrast to the militarized U.S. side — colorless double fences with razor wire, drones overhead, Border Patrol vehicles dragging the sand to make footprints apparent. Yet even on the U.S. side, in between the two sections of fence, a short distance from the ocean lies Friendship Park, originally dedicated by First Lady Pat Nixon in the 1970s. Here families divided by the border sometimes meet briefly and emotionally under Border Patrol supervision. For many years, pastors on both sides of the border have prayed together each Sunday through the fence. Just before Christmas, people gather on both sides for the Mexican custom of the *Las Posadas*, a singing procession about Mary and Joseph searching for a place of hospitality as Jesus is about to be born in Bethlehem. One year when I went, the authorities moved people so far back from the fence that we could not hear the singing from the other side.

The border fence serves as a canvas not only for art but for theological questions as well, questions about fear and hospitality, unity and division, sorrow and hope. It reminds us that migration as a human phenomenon cannot but raise basic questions about God, human life, and the reach of human community. Theology as a discipline prides itself on addressing these questions. They demand that we reflect not just on how people ought to *behave* toward migrants, either interpersonally or as a nation, but also what migration means in the light of Christian faith. In this chapter, we see that migration provokes different interpretations from different theologians for varied reasons. Some begin by looking at traditional Christian doctrines in a slightly different way, using migration as a lens or metaphor. Others, especially those with direct experience accompanying undocumented or marginalized migrants, focus on the suffering undocumented migrants—men and women—are made to endure and how that suffering echoes the mystery of Jesus's death and resurrection. Others, attentive to border fences and the politics of restriction, look to the ancient Christian theology (and practice) of hospitality. These different theological approaches to migration will set us up for the conclusion of the book, when we squarely face migration as a theological tension or paradox.

THE MIGRANT GOD

The theologian Peter Phan, himself a refugee from Vietnam, starts his account of a theology of migration from the ancient Christian dogma of the Holy Trinity, that is, the central teaching of one God in three persons. Until recent years, the theology of the Trinity had fallen on hard times, making it seem oddly esoteric and disconnected for a core belief.[3] Following a renewal of Trinitarian theology in recent decades, however, Phan speaks of the Trinity in terms of God's movement into the world out of love. He sees the Son coming into the world in Jesus of Nazareth and God the Holy Spirit dwelling in the world as manifestations of *Deus migrator,* a migrant God. Jesus becomes the paradigmatic migrant, refused hospitality at the moment of his birth, a child refugee in Egypt, an itinerant preacher, a guest in others' houses, one who never ceased to reach across metaphorical borders to invite in marginal persons, and one who crossed the boundaries of life, death, and resurrection. The Holy Spirit dwells in our world as an immigrant force "pushing history toward the fulfillment of the kingdom of God."[4] All people and indeed all creation move inexorably toward that ultimate fulfillment of perfect unity, peace, justice, and love. In short, Creation is a kind of migrant journey in the hands of a migrant God.[5]

Therefore, Phan argues, the earthly migrant of today is a privileged and visible image of God, an *imago Dei migratoris.* Of course, in Christian theology, all human beings are created in the image of God, endowing them with a dignity that cannot be taken away. But like the God who leaves the "safety of God's eternal home to the strange and risky land of the human family,"[6] the migrant knows the vulnerability and transience of human life perhaps better than the average citizen. And just as God's entrance into human life does not take away the transcendent holiness of God, so too migration does not rob the migrant of their dignity before God. Thus, Phan goes so far as to say, echoing Jesus identifying, in Matthew 25:35, with the Christian stranger:

> Thus, when the migrant is embraced, protected, and loved, the *Deus Migrator* is embraced, protected, and loved. By the same token, when the migrant as *imago Dei migratoris* is rejected, marginalized, declared "illegal," imprisoned, tortured, or killed, it is the original of that image, the *Deus Migrator*, who is subjected to the same inhuman and sinful treatment.[7]

In this way, Phan argues that a Christian theology of a "migrant God" has concrete implications for actual migrants. Other theologians, however, begin the theological process in reverse. They start with the actual experience of migration and then move toward theological principles and conclusions, what in theology is generally called a "theology from below."

MIGRANTS AND THE CROSS

Recent trips to the border with my students bring us face-to-face with the stories of Mexican deportees and Central Americans seeking asylum. Hearing the stories of all that they had endured—parents or children with desperate needs back at home; the murders of family members and friends in Central American cities; dangerous journeys across Mexico atop the infamous freight train *La Bestia* (the beast); and forced separation from spouses and young children after decades in the United States—even the most skeptical of my students feel compassion and empathy. When I go for a longer trip with graduate students, we often visit the small-town cemetery in the Imperial Valley of California, where migrants who die crossing the desert are buried, including many whose grave markers simply say, "Jane Doe" or "John Doe," since they were never identified. I recall one of my students placing a small cross next to a grave. Someone had inked "God is with us" on the cross in bright red marker. Amid all the suffering, almost anyone could be led to wonder how this could be so.

Yet several theologians have taken pains to assert that God is indeed with those who suffer on their migration journeys. One of the foremost U.S. theologians of migration is Daniel Groody, a Euro-American Holy Cross priest who teaches at the University of Notre Dame. He has spoken with migrants all over the world, but his first theology of migration still speaks powerfully of what human beings endure when they cross borders, a product of his time working with immigrant farm laborers in the Coachella Valley of California. On one end of that valley, people of Mexican and Central American origin work the land in the hot desert sun for low wages, often living in sub-standard conditions. On the other end, wealthy retirees play golf and sit under mist sprays in the courtyards of restaurants. In between lies the huge fairgrounds that hosts the annual Coachella Music Festival, attended by a large number of my undergraduate students.

Groody explains the dynamics of suffering for undocumented Mexican Catholics who take part in retreats offered through the Valley Missionary Program. He speaks of the pressures to leave home, the painful separations, the dangers of a journey that for some ends in death in a canal or in the desert. Groody also outlines three distinct forms of alienation that such migrants feel — political and cultural alienation as rejected "aliens" in a foreign land; socioeconomic alienation as they remain poor, doing hard, despised work in a wealthy land; and psycho-spiritual alienation. "Loneliness is a heavy burden and one of the most unrecognized aspects of the immigrant's pain," Groody writes.[8] The "crushed hearts" of migrants mirror the painful crucifixion of Jesus, revealing the oppressive dynamics of power around migration, the sacrifices people make for their families, and the way God's presence emerges in a special way at the margins of society.[9] But Groody goes on to show how these crushed hearts are healed and animated by a holistic process of ritual and personal conversion facilitated by the retreats. These immigrants shake off negative images of themselves, sexist notions about gender, and harsh images of God. They find their way to a new celebration of their own value as persons, the value of their often-depreciated culture, and the value of their faith in God. In this way, they live Jesus's own resurrection.[10]

Other theologians also take up the metaphor of crucifixion to help us reflect on suffering at the border, including Giaocchino

Campese, an Italian priest of the migrant-serving Scalabrini Catholic religious order, and Nancy Pineda-Madrid, a Catholic systematic theologian, originally from the borderlands of El Paso. Both specifically engage the theological symbol of the "crucified people." This theological symbol emerged from the work of Jesuit Ignacio Ellacuría, who was martyred in 1989 as part of a campaign of state-sponsored violence in El Salvador. In the context of a long history of deep poverty and political violence in his adopted country, Ellacuría saw all around him a crucified people, that is, a marginalized, poor community compelled to bear suffering imposed by the powerful. The crucified people were like the Suffering Servant in the biblical Book of Isaiah, a collective embodiment of the way the powerless both expose and carry the sins of their oppressors. They echo the crucified Christ, and like him, they become instruments of salvation for the rest by exposing wrongdoing and demanding an end to it, or in Ellacuría's colleague Jon Sobrino's memorable phrase, "taking the crucified people down from the Cross."[11]

Campese describes how those who attempt to cross the border without papers are the targets of the institutionalized violence of U.S. border control since the late 1980s. Since then, federal governments led by both political parties have pursued a strategy of deterrence where they intentionally pushed unauthorized immigrants to cross the border in the most inhospitable and dangerous places, producing a death toll now well over seven thousand by the Border Patrol's own figures.[12] According to Campese, when U.S. Christians fail to recognize this crucifixion, that is, "if they consider the deaths of the immigrants 'as simply a fact of life'—the 'collateral damage' that necessarily comes with the 'sacred' duty to protect the border from invaders and terrorists—then they are contributing, even if unwillingly, to the crucifixion at the U.S.–Mexico border."[13]

Pineda-Madrid draws specific attention to women who suffer at the border, either through sex trafficking or via feminicide, a "crucifixion of females as females" that "fundamentally challenges the definition of a crucified people."[14] The Mexican cultural anthropologist Olivia Ruiz Marrujo also reminds us of the widespread sexual violence inflicted on Mexican women hoping to cross the border and especially Central American migrant women crossing through Mexico.[15] Pineda-Madrid shows how the suffering of these *mujeres desechables* ("disposable women") is routinely dismissed, ignored, or forgotten, simply because they are women. That dismissal or forgetting requires that Christians repair the damage, that they "re-member the mystical body of Christ so as to include these dead" and suffering.[16] But the metaphor of the crucified people demands not only that all of us recognize the humanity and suffering of these overlooked persons.but also more controversially that we see them as instruments of our own salvation, calling us to account, demanding that we see them as a part of us and *respond* to their suffering by taking action in their defense — taking them down from the cross.[17]

These theologies of suffering bring necessary attention to largely invisible and powerless parts of the migrant population. By connecting that suffering to the suffering and death of Jesus, these scholars locate migrant suffering at the center of Christian life, interpreting it through that core mystery. At least one theologian warns us about the potential "spiritualizing" of migrant suffering as a result: "To romanticize migration and canonize those among us who migrate is to dehumanize and disregard the particularity of each life."[18] Groody maintains, however, that connecting the suffering of migrants to the mystery of Christ's death and resurrection as memorialized in the Christian Eucharist keeps us from trivializing the brutal mystery at the center of Christian life. "When one loses a sense of the integral relationship between the body of Christ in the Eucharist and the bodies of those who suffer in the world, the Christian life suffers, degenerating into concern over form without substance, law without spirit, and rules without heart."[19]

Generalized connections can also turn our attention away from the people and structures that *inflict* migrant suffering, as Pineda-Madrid and Campese remind us. Pineda-Madrid's attention to the suffering inflicted on women *because they are women* points to an aspect of migrant suffering alluded to but not fully considered in the other theologies of suffering. The threat narrative of immigration considered in chapter 3 does not so much target immigrants for being immigrants as for being Mexican or Latin American. Even the rule of law cultural narrative about immigration, which divides good and bad immigrants, nearly always has Mexican or Central American immigrants in mind for the latter. As also noted in chapter 3, unauthorized Mexican and Central American migrants are dismissed, deported, and dehumanized more easily and more noisily, not just because of their legal status, but also because they are not white. In short, the immigrant "bodies of those who suffer in the world" (in Groody's words) suffer in large part because their bodies are brown.

Black liberation theologians like the late James Cone or the Catholic Shawn Copeland do not shrink from the fact that African American suffering is inflicted because of bodily features like skin color, which cannot be discarded when connecting their suffering to that of Christ.[20] Theologies of immigrant suffering must also attend to the racialized roots of inhospitality to immigrants. In a sense, we encounter here a distinct racist cultural narrative that impacts migration: In the United States, lighter skin color and European facial features are read by many people as somehow more naturally "American." This narrative troubles not only Latin American immigrants today but other nonwhite immigrants, such as Haitians. It troubled many groups in the past, including Chinese or Japanese immigrants, or even Irish and Italian immigrants and Ashkenazi Jews, all visually portrayed in ways that distinguished them from other people of European origin. This same hostility to outsiders of certain backgrounds also points us in a different theological direction. How can nations like the United States, with a strong Christian heritage, have paid so little attention to the ancient Christian theology and practice of hospitality?

THEOLOGIES OF HOSPITALITY

When I was ten or eleven, my parents and their friends formed a couples' "Gourmet Club" and traded off hosting dinner parties. Many years later, this sounds like a marvelous idea, but at the time I did not welcome the occasions. The Saturdays when my parents hosted, they would be busy cooking and concocting signature cocktails, and my siblings and I were set to work cleaning the house—vacuuming, dusting, cleaning bathrooms and windows. The best towels came out in the bathrooms. More care was shown to setting the table and arranging snacks in the living room. As the evening began, we also made an appearance to greet my parents' guests. After that, our main job was to steer clear of the adults and occupy ourselves without causing any trouble. Looking back, I see that my mother used these occasions to impart lessons and habits of hospitality to us. Welcoming guests meant cleaning the house, preparing food and drink, setting out the nicer amenities, and personally greeting those who came.

All human cultures have their customs and habits of hospitality. The English word *hospitality* traces its roots back to the Latin term *hospitalitem*, which means "friendliness to guests." As was noted in chapter 7, however, the earliest Christians had a more expansive take on hospitality, that it should be extended not just to friends or the elite but to strangers and poor persons. "Rather than entertaining persons who had something to offer, and thereby gaining advantage from their hospitality, Christians were deliberately to welcome those who seemingly brought little to the encounter."[21] Thus, one of the New Testament words often translated as hospitality is *philoxenia*, which literally means "love of the stranger."[22] Theologian Ana Maria Pineda, an immigrant from El Salvador, sees the Latin American custom of the *Las Posadas* as a nearly perfect symbolic embodiment of hospitality, with its reenactment in song and practice of the pregnant Virgin Mary and Joseph her husband arriving in Bethlehem as strangers seeking shelter.[23] Pineda describes hospitality as "the practice of providing a space where the stranger is taken in and known as one who bears gifts."[24]

The Evangelical biblical scholar Joshua Jipp argues that Christian hospitality is a foundational response to God's hospitality to us. In various New Testament texts in Luke and Acts, St. Paul's letters, and the Gospel of John, Jipp observes Jesus acting as a host serving up divine hospitality to a world of outsiders.[25] Christians should imitate Christ by welcoming immigrants and refugees who by definition have been cut off from family, culture, and home. He draws particular attention to God's hospitality to Israel as an immigrant people in the Hebrew Bible: "Israel conceptualizes itself perpetually as immigrants, sojourners, and guests before God and as a people whose existence is sustained by God's hospitality. God loves Israel *because* God loves the immigrant."[26] As an Evangelical Christian, Jipp is clear how this biblical message contradicts and confronts the xenophobic rhetoric of many conservative Christians, but he also points to many voices of compassion among Evangelicals. He urges Christians to judge the rhetoric of political leaders by this biblical message rather than by ideological leanings, and to especially reject anti-immigrant rhetoric with a racist tint. He further asks Christians to become more educated about immigration and to welcome immigrants and refugees to their particular churches.[27]

This relatively straightforward exhortation to hospitality toward migrants is complicated in the work of other theologians. Catholic Carmen Nanko-Fernández and Protestant Nell Becker Sweeden, the latter a theologian from the Holiness Wesleyan tradition, both draw attention to the power dynamics implicit in hospitality: Nanko-Fernández says that in most instances of church hospitality, "We are church and *they* are the stranger. We make an option for them....The power resides on the side of the one who has the ability to choose to welcome or to turn away."[28] Sweeden admits that in Christian history too often hospitality was used "as a force for assimilation into a particular homogeneous way of life that neglects to value the contributions of the stranger, outsider, or Other, and often inflicts harm upon them."[29] She points to critical theory in philosophy, where hospitality is described as necessitating that the stranger make demands and incur a debt to the host. Equality or true relationship remain impossible.[30]

Nanko-Fernández sees clearly how this power asymmetry remains largely unexamined by members of a receiving community. They do not question their ownership over the local community (or the nation). In one parish I studied, for example, longtime locals saw no problem with their complete custody over the decoration of the church for Christmas, even though they shared that church with a large immigrant Mexican community. Often inertia plays a role in such unquestioned ownership, but too often it has an implicit racial basis. White Americans often see their own place in communities and institutions as natural and right, and thus we think we have the right to act as gatekeepers over people from other racial or ethnic groups. We must be honest with the difficult truth: the true name of this kind of racial normativity is white supremacy. Its assumptions and logic can entrap immigrant Christians of color as well when, despite their baptism and belonging, they find themselves eternal guests.

Not surprisingly, then, the Pentecostal theologian Amos Yong argues that true Christian hospitality requires *metanoia*, a change in how people see the world. In Catholic social teaching, the world's goods are destined for all people, the foundation of the Catholic idea of the right to migrate. But human beings often think of the world in stingier terms, where even in a land of plenty everything is presumed to be scarce, calling for strict norms of reciprocity (or even the need to hoard). Various cultural narratives about immigration employ metaphors of "invasion" or "inundation" (flood) or traffic in inaccurate associations between migrants and crime. All this rhetoric relies on an empirically inaccurate perspective of scarcity. Yong encourages us to shift instead to a worldview emphasizing God's abundance. In response, "the host can continually give herself away without losing herself."[31] Such a perspective, Yong argues, allows the "stranger" to hold to a distinct and different identity even as host and stranger gather together in community or worship. The host does not need to remake the stranger in their image to assuage the host's fear. All are made in God's image, but *distinctively* so. But such uniqueness, according to theologian Mayra Rivera, is not one of absolute autonomy but forged in relationships. I am distinctively me as a product of my relationships with others, including with those labeled as "stranger."[32]

At its best then, the church becomes a "borderland," where identity is constantly renegotiated and rediscovered in these relationships. There is no need for strangers to assimilate to some presumed inherited static identity. God continues to re-create us into new people through our encounters with one another. "In a sense, borderlands also are spaces in which everyone is encountered as a stranger."[33] The Catholic theologian Gemma Tulud Cruz, a Philippine immigrant to Australia, echoes this idea by speaking of a "church of the stranger," where God is the only true host:

> Imaging God as the host provides a way of not falling into the trap of paternalistic hospitality. Seeing God as the provider of hospitality destabilizes the usual roles (with the migrant as the usual guest and the citizen as the usual host) and the unbalanced order of relations these roles spawn. God as the host presents, instead, both the migrant and the citizen as guests, and consequently, as both strangers.[34]

Our encounters with one another, then, at their best, remind us that no citizen (or Christian) is chosen by God to enjoy some sort of special privilege relative to others. The Christian is chosen only insomuch as they are called by God to gather everyone into a world of greater equity and justice.[35] True Christian hospitality, then, does not divide us into hosts with control and guests or strangers with vulnerable need. It recognizes the vulnerable need in all of us on our common journey.[36]

THEOLOGIES OF MIGRATION

Theologies of migration, like those presented here, require the same sort of critical attention as the cultural narratives examined in chapters 3 and 4. There is always the worry that strong advocacy for a particular understanding of migration in theology will turn into a kind of "one true story" that leaves little room for argument or, even worse, that excludes some people's migration stories simply because they do not fit the theology. Thus we examined a variety of approaches here, from Peter Phan's more "top-down" theology of a migrant God (*Deus Migrator*) to theologies relating migrants' suffering to the death and resurrection of Jesus (and making them his "crucified people"), concluding with theologies rooted in the ancient Christian practice and theology of hospitality. All these approaches have rough edges. Phan's notion of the Christian God as a migrant has a creative edge to it, but it only responds to the concerns of contemporary migrants in a general and abstract way. Theologies of the cross center on the very real suffering of undocumented immigrants, usually those men and women who cross the border without papers, but they often miss both the racial component to that suffering and the burdens of other types of immigrants. Finally, ancient notions of Christian hospitality require that we work through the unequal power dynamics often implicit in them.

Every theology (and ethics) of migration has its lights and shadows, its strong points and weak points, its targeted context that cannot address every migrant's story. This effectively makes it impossible to weave together all the different theological and ethical approaches scattered throughout this text. Instead, in the conclusion, I will make a few observations not only about what we have learned about migration but also about what is still missing. Those observations set us up for a modest proposal of what people of good will might do in practice to respect the human dignity of migrants, while also moving closer to just and reasonable receiving communities.

Chapter Ten

CONCLUSION

A Practical Theology of Migration

Students in my courses on migration, especially those who do not identify as religious, are often surprised to hear a theology professor spending so much time addressing cultural narratives, or family memories about migration, or the history of the Great Migration, let alone the sociology of migration and adaptation. Often their internal definition of *religion* or *theology* was shaped by childhood experiences that identified organized religion with a moralistic or doctrinaire approach. As a result, many of my students find it both refreshing and surprising that a college theology course not only takes a wide-ranging, open approach to the subject of migration, but that it also affords space to examine big questions that come up in their other courses, questions about suffering, human rights, racial and ethnic discrimination, and ethical responsibility.

The interdisciplinary and wide-ranging approach across this text is intentional. This methodological approach from pastoral or practical theology takes specific interest in how theological scholarship and religious traditions *shape and are shaped* by the questions and practices of everyday life, inside and outside of faith communities, or what Latinx theologians refer to as *lo cotidiano*.[1] Practical theology methodologies require serious social analysis of the current situation, and so in this textbook, we started by looking at theory and data from the historical and sociological study of migration, as well as various cultural narratives that migrants and receiving community members use to interpret migration. That social analysis in turn informed the theological reflection that ensued, which had to be both historically savvy and appreciative of contemporary dilemmas. Thus, we grounded the Christian theological exploration of migration by locating it among that of other religious traditions, especially the other Abrahamic traditions, which also see migration as part of their foundations. We looked at the biblical roots of Christian perspectives on migration, including the constant presence of migrants throughout the Bible, protections afforded migrants in the Torah or Pentateuch, the itineracy of Jesus and his early followers, and some of the "difficult passages" around migration, such as Romans 13. We then traced how migration and hospitality to migrants changed throughout Christian history, concluding that chapter with the rise of Catholic social teaching at the turn of the twentieth century. Just as biblical foundations proved influential for Protestant ethics, Catholic social teaching provided foundational principles for Catholic ethical reflection on migration. While a few ethicists argue for strong borders, most think the status quo around migration has become insufficiently appreciative of the predicaments of especially unauthorized immigrants today. Finally, we carefully examined the thinking of contemporary Christian theologians on migration, with particular attention to theologies of suffering and hospitality.

Readers exposed to more judgmental and doctrinaire experiences of religion may, like my students, find themselves a little stunned that so much of ethics and theology has an inclusive and pro-migrant tenor to it. At the same time, the variety of different kinds of reflection in ethics and theology can be uncomfortably broad and varied. In these pages we have wandered our way through ethical reflections that alternately emphasized prioritizing citizens, the unity of humanity, human rights, family integrity, a preference for the suffering poor, and responsibility that comes from concrete historical relationships. We have seen theologies of hospitality, of suffering, and of God the migrant, with some theologies taking issue with the assumptions of other theologies. There is, in the end, no realistic way to tie all these loose ends together, and I will make no attempt to do so. Instead, I ask leave to move only in the most general way in the direction of a practical theology of migration, touching on a few lessons from our journey together, mainly about the cultural narratives that often shape our discourse and practice around migration. The limitations of these narratives will lead us to important, unresolved tensions and persistent questions. Finally, we conclude with practical suggestions for a reform of our everyday practice in the real world or, in other words, suggestions for well-intentioned people longing for a better world, whether or not they are religious.

BEYOND CULTURAL NARRATIVES

Perhaps the most important lesson of this comprehensive examination of migration is that the cultural narratives people employ to understand migration, whether they have their origins in receiving, migrant, or sending communities, often prove inadequate. For example, immigrant threat narratives, or narratives of resentment against migrants in sending communities, necessarily view migration as out of the ordinary, as something strange and morally suspect. The land belongs to the nation whose borders enclose it; people should stay where they are. But they do not, and they never have. In these pages we encountered migration as a constant social fact. Migration first appeared in prehistoric times, later in the Bible and Qur'an, across the history of various religions, across U.S. history, up until and including today's world. Most of the time, borders have been shown to be more porous than locked down. Migration is not strange or suspect, but constant and normal.

Other cultural narratives—the better life, the better deal, the rule of law, escape—may provide limited insight into a particular type of migration experience, or into the nuances of distinct communities' interpretations of that experience, but they still come up short when we examine the complex historical and empirical realities of immigration. They fail to respond to some of the more important moral demands of religious teaching. None of the cultural narratives we explored remains broad enough to account even for the four ideal types of immigrants identified in chapter 2: professionals, laborers, entrepreneurs, and refugees. Even regarding refugees and escape, it turns out that not all who needed to escape persecution found welcome, and many whose descendants claimed they escaped persecution actually did not. Even the supposedly iron line between legal and illegal migration turns out to be more fluid than most people believe. Most undocumented people in the United States, for example, actually came with legal visas and then overstayed them, and people move in and out of status in ways only lawyers really understand. Stereotypes about unauthorized migrants as unstable or criminal have usually proven incorrect. To sum up, none of the cultural narratives suffices because there is no "one true story," no migration metanarrative, that can account for all of it.[2]

This also reminds us that migrants and their stories cannot be reduced to categories or archetypes. They are *people* with families and relationships, emotions, complex dreams, theories about life, and (to Christians) the grace of God operating within them. Each one of these persons has an innate dignity that Christians and Jews tie to their being made in God's image, but that is also asserted by the United Nations Declaration on Human Rights: "All human beings are born free and equal in dignity and rights" (article 1). My fondest hope is that the readers of this book find out what most of my students come to see: migrants, refugees, and deportees are human beings who deserve empathy and a hearing. When that is not clear, or when politicians or pundits purposefully mask that truth with manipulative arguments or dehumanizing rhetoric, it becomes a simple thing to vote for mass deportations, to break up families, and to make no connection between migrants and one's basic faith commitments or ethical principles. I recognize that readers may come to different conclusions about the politics of immigration law, but I hope all of us never forget that migration is primarily about *people*.

The people involved include not only migrants but the citizens of both receiving and sending communities. It is fair to consider the needs of both, though not to the exclusion of migrants. Even as we respect all parties, we have to ask hard questions about the impact of migration on sending communities, both positively (remittances, global economic networks, cultural exchanges) and negatively (brain drain, personal loss). We must also acknowledge that receiving communities are changed, even re-created by the waves of migration, whether those waves be international or internal migrants.[3] The intercultural encounters that ensue can be stressful and anxiety-producing for all; change is hard. Patience is required while people grieve what is lost, and encouragement is needed while they accommodate their new world. While demographic changes often terrify people, sometimes disgracefully because they tap into long-held—though sometimes buried—racial or ethnic fears and bias, in real life, demographic change does not spell disaster for migrants or receiving communities. Human beings are resilient. As my track coach brother-in-law would say, good players adjust.

HUMAN TENSIONS

On most pages of this study, the view of migration remained close-up. Historical accounts, sociological analysis, the presentation of narratives, and biblical, ethical, and theological commentary all have their own approaches and patterns, and they are often quite different. Still, the comprehensive nature of this text, and the practical theology methodologies employed, do permit us a moment to step back and look at the whole thing. Part of what that clarifies is that migration brings out the essential ambiguity of human experience. We are generous, distrustful, hospitable, naïve, idealistic, and casually cruel beings. Migration exposes the moral tensions in human life. In this way, it is like standing at the western edge of the U.S.–Mexico border with my students. Looking all around one sees the sparkling water and the imposing fence, the markers of international friendship and of suspicion, the big beautiful murals and the menacing gray razor wire.

Thus, on the one hand, we have seen how the general arc of Christian theology bends toward hospitality. Perhaps no leader embodies this better than Pope Francis. His first trip as pope was to the island of Lampedusa, an Italian outpost halfway to North Africa and the site of many camps for rescued African migrants. Over and over, Pope Francis has encouraged a "culture of encounter" in our world, which he identifies with an openness to finding God in other people through diverse experiences and perspectives. The word *encuentro* in the pope's native Spanish implies a serendipitous, joyful, and transformative exchange, which is something more than just running into someone. He worries that the efficiency of modern life too often pushes us past one another into indifference, so that eventually "there is no place for the elderly or for the unwanted child; there is no time for that poor person in the street."[4] He urges us to approach all our encounters, especially with those who are different, with patient openness and a willingness to be changed for the better.

We find no figure of the international stature of Pope Francis outspokenly *opposed* to more hospitality to immigrants. The American Evangelical preacher Franklin Graham, son of the iconic evangelist Billy Graham, however, has been outspoken in his antagonism against the immigration of Muslims to the United States. "We are under attack by Muslims at home and abroad," he argued, and he has consistently engaged in anti-Islamic rhetoric since 2001.[5] But the most consistent and most vehement use of anti-immigrant rhetoric has come not from clergy but from *political* leaders who identify as white Evangelicals or white Catholics. They repeat the cultural narratives of threat or draw strict moral lines between legal and illegal immigration. Migrants or refugees become criminal invaders rather than people. This rhetoric may provide those who espouse it with a sense of order and protection, but it also makes the "culture of encounter" Pope Francis encourages next to impossible. The rhetoric makes it easy to treat not just unauthorized but large swaths of immigrants as nonpersons, turning them into the "crucified peoples" we heard about in the previous chapter. Migration is already difficult, with its dramatic moves from culture to culture. People mourn what they have lost. Adaptation requires decades of exposure and commitment, and such adaptation may only find completion in the journey of the second or third generation. Rhetoric that obscures the humanity of migrants and refugees inflicts pain and prolongs the adaptation process by pushing people away from one another.

Indeed, on an even deeper level, migration exposes the tension between our drive toward human unity and our propensity to tear our communities apart. On the one hand, migration points like a compass toward the way our separate geographies do not have to determine our destiny. Migration indicates a trajectory toward what Pope John XXIII more than half a century ago called "the unity of the human family" (*Pacem in Terris* 132). One image that never leaves me is in the moments before a Catholic parish council meeting began in a divided parish, where middle-aged and elderly white pastoral council members delightedly held and cooed around the new baby of a young immigrant couple. I felt that I had witnessed the common humanity of people with different positions, cultures, and languages. It was a tiny signal of the way Catholics see their religion as a global communion, a web of relationship uniting diverse peoples, and at least potentially a sacrament of human unity (*Lumen Gentium* 1), even as that unity remains tarnished and unfinished in our world.

Migration as a phenomenon also unveils, however, the stubborn need of human beings to be right and the concurrent proclivity to dehumanize those who disagree. It reveals the fear of what is different and even the profoundly irrational hatred that disrupts our fragile trajectory toward unity. At our own peril, we ignore the fact that much of the human story of immigration in these pages is a story of inhospitality and resistance, from the biblical persecution of Tobit and Anna noted in the first chapter, to the racial epithets Asian and Pacific Islander friends received on city streets during the coronavirus crisis in 2020. Many immigrants today and yesterday could tell stories about the way their employers exploited them because they knew they could not object or complain. I can picture the bumper stickers from my hometown from decades ago that declared about a local enclave for Southeast Asian refugees, "Will the last American to leave please take the flag?" Once, after hearing a particularly harrowing tale of discrimination, I related the whole story to my parish's office manager. "Why would someone do that?" I asked, infuriated. Without hesitation, he simply answered, "Sin?" Indeed, the story of migration is as much a record of human evil as it is a compass pointing toward unity. Or perhaps it functions more like a high-definition television screen, magnifying what is both beautiful and ugly within us.

BORDERS AND NATIONS

The high-definition display that is migration not only magnifies the good and bad in our humanity; it also magnifies the morally ambiguous, often absurd world of international borders. Years ago, my wife took a group of students to see the border fence. Their guide from a local nonprofit organization began to poke his hand in and out of the gap between the large metal fence posts, declaring in a comical voice, "Okay, I am in Mexico. No, I am in the United States. Wait, I am in Mexico." On one of my trips to the border fence by the ocean, a student pointed toward the fence heading into the surf and wondered aloud if dolphins and seals had to show their papers. Borders matter a great deal in the lives of citizens and immigrants, but they are not part of nature, were not handed down by God. Human beings put them there, often after painful and violent struggles.

Borders do, however, mark off the nation-state system that governs much of our lives. The elegant utility of that system cannot be denied; it divides the entire world into distinct states with distinct governments, each fully sovereign within its borders, at least allegedly. Rights are apportioned to human beings via their citizenship in one of these bordered states. In real life, however, that elegant utility can break down. Failed states are countries in name only; civil wars divide sovereignty between groups; racial, ethnic, and gender discrimination decide who really has rights; multinational corporations possess unchecked and powerful influence; and organized crime cartels, armed gangs, and feuding warlords serve in no government but have effective control. Millions of people around the world permanently settle in countries where they have no legal status, in many cases with little hope for ever acquiring those rights that citizenship bestows. Some even become effectively or legally "stateless," without any citizenship at all.[6]

Despite these failures of the nation-state system, the delineating of it through international borders has a strong hold on us. In practical reality, borders are products of history, of specific wars and treaties. They could easily have been otherwise. But borders *feel* to us like a given, a matter of common sense, a taken-for-granted reality. People often project onto borders not only a legal but a moral authority. Borders are presumed to divide jurisdiction from jurisdiction, country from country, and also to divide stability from chaos, or even friend from enemy. Persons on the other side of a border move quickly from being seen as potential tourists or visitors into invaders and criminals, as certain cultural narratives designate them. Even more hospitable cultural narratives, such as those who presume that immigrants yearn for a "better life," appear to position the destination country as somehow inherently better. A better life implies an intrinsically rather than merely a strategically better place.

Upon reflection, the careful observer recognizes that such conclusions about the moral superiority on one side of a border are assumed rather than well reasoned. My own students repeatedly remind me that borders have an arbitrary quality to them, that one could just as easily have been born on one side as the other. Because of our emotional attachment to our cultures and countries, we want our citizenship to bestow on us special status or moral importance. But philosophically speaking, citizenship is an accident of birth, or perhaps of circumstance. Borders, especially in their current configuration, have no innate or absolute *moral* significance. They do not of necessity divide good people from bad people, only people from other people. Border controls furthermore can operate in ways that are unjust, punitive, even dangerous, as, for example, when deterrence policies lead to deadly journeys through the desert or when continued detention during a pandemic puts immigrants with health vulnerabilities at severe risk.[7]

The complex story of migration in these pages suggests that, instead of investing borders with a significant role in the moral order, we might simply recognize their role in the social order. Indeed, even those who propose totally "open borders" would probably acknowledge that borders remain administratively necessary. The city limits of Los Angeles, where I live, designate which fire department or street paving unit is responsible for which neighborhoods. National borders similarly designate who lives under what constitution, or what institutions serve what constituencies. Rather than moral significance, borders offer jurisdiction. They do not always do so justly, and that fact deserves our attention. But no one in Southern California will assert in any serious way that Angelenos, that is, L.A. residents, are somehow better or more deserving than those that live in Culver City or another adjacent suburb. The fire department does not judge me unworthy of their help because, even though I live in Los Angeles, I was not born or raised there.

MIGRATION AND PRACTICE

If originating on one side or the other of a national border confers no automatic moral superiority, then neither are people on either side absolved from the responsibility to see that borders, citizenship, and migration work justly, in a way that respects the human dignity of migrants and citizens. I invite us to now move from the theory that is customary in book group discussions and university classes and back to the question of action and practice. What kind of things should persons of good will, religious or not, *do* on a regular and repeated basis to move us toward a better and more just world for migrants, sending communities, and receiving communities? As a way of concluding this book, I offer six recommendations.

First, especially in a polarized society, migration invites us to listen—to migrants, to deportees, to members of receiving and sending communities. In the first chapters, I explained how I learned about the heartbreaking stories of refugees from Haiti and deportees separated from their families. So often we do not really listen but wait for other people to say either what confirms our beliefs or offends us because it does not. This, in a fundamental way, is the problem with many cultural narratives. They condition us to come to a predetermined conclusion, often far afield from migrants' actual experiences. To listen carefully is to learn about another person's experience according to their own view of that experience. This is not easy. I once heard a Border Patrol agent dismiss the truth of the stories of Central American refugees fleeing gang violence. They were liars, nothing more. I realized that some narrative in his head required that they be liars. But what if he had listened to them with an open mind? He may not have changed his mind about his job to enforce immigration laws, but he perhaps would have done so with more empathy and respect. In fact, I have seen other Border Patrol agents do exactly that, and these moments begin to manifest Pope Francis's "culture of encounter."

Second, it should be abundantly clear that people of good will cannot engage in, encourage, or even accept in their presence the depersonalizing anti-immigrant rhetoric of recent times. Much of that rhetoric has a subtle—sometimes not-so-subtle—racist tinge to it. Does anyone really use "illegals" to talk about Poles or Canadians? Even as citizens negotiate disagreements about who should be allowed to enter and in what numbers, even as migrants and citizens dispute how they should share communities, we have to use words that regard the other as a person, not a problem. I work to respect different viewpoints in my classes and conversations—more successfully as I have gained experience as a teacher—but I also insist that teacher and students employ accurate and person-centered terminology. This is a matter not of political correctness but of respect.

This brings us to our third practice: I would urge us to practice skepticism in the face of all cultural narratives about migration. Threat narratives speak of "scofflaws" and "criminals" and "anchor babies." Even before we investigate how well these accusations fit with empirical data (they do not, see chapter 3), we ought to begin by asking why they are only leveled at people from Mexico or Central America. Why are Muslim immigrants so often suspected of being terrorists when homegrown, white supremacist terrorists are far more numerous? Even the most positive-sounding cultural narratives—that people come to seek a better life or to escape persecution—require scrutiny. Do poor labor immigrants expect that they will encounter a better life, or just marginally better pay or working conditions? Does our defense of those who suffer religious persecution apply only to certain religions? Do our political views make us sympathetic only to some refugees but not others? Our fidelity to truth and to our own codes of ethics—religiously based or not—insists that we ask these difficult questions.

These three practices enable a fourth, more challenging practice, that of hospitality. When I went to study Spanish in Guadalajara in Mexico decades ago, my host mother was unfailingly polite, curious about me, and generous in her explanations of Mexican customs or culture. She always called me with kindness to eat, and her food was delicious. She did all these things without a hint of condescension or paternalism, though I was inexperienced in the life of her homeland. Thinking of Doña Tere all those years ago makes me attentive to my own hospitality to others, especially to immigrants recently arrived. Perhaps whenever citizens get in touch with gratitude for the good in their own lives, for the hospitality they have received, they practice welcome. It is, however, not one's own sense of gratitude that demands such welcome but rather the dignity of immigrants as persons. It is not required that the welcomed immigrant has a story that reads as legitimate according to one's politics or is from a category that the citizen sees as optimal for admission. An immigrant stands before a citizen as a person, not a position. I am struck again by the Torah commandments to welcome the *ger*, or alien, which almost always made reference to the Israelites' bad experiences as *gerim* in Egypt. Part of hospitality, after all, is recognizing our own vulnerability: that any of us could be, under the right circumstances, stranger or alien.

Both listening and welcoming allow us to engage in a fifth practice. During the coronavirus pandemic lockdowns in 2020, it became perhaps clearer to many middle-class people how dependent they were on the "essential workers" that harvest their food, stock store shelves, check them out at the market, build and renovate their houses, care for their landscapes, or clean up after them. Many of the people who do this work are in fact migrants, often poor laborers of some sort. In private and public ways, citizens need to appreciate this work that sustains their lives, done by immigrants and internal migrants within North America. Too often, these "essential workers" are treated as inferior beings, parts in the grand economic machine. In terms of respect, courtesy, kindness, and just remuneration, appreciation for their contribution is more than warranted.

Finally, I have learned as a professor that some students will study migration and then take what they have learned to heart by engaging in even more dramatic practices. I can remember one of the first times I taught a unit on migration in a graduate course, and another time when I spoke about it to parishioners in a Catholic parish. In each case, I shared stories and, more important, invited people to share stories with one another. Moved by what they heard, some of the native-born citizens in the groups became advocates and activists. Such persons call, write, or visit legislators in search of reform. They argue with their friends and families. They bus to demonstrations. Some, especially fellow immigrants, conduct "know your rights" workshops for undocumented immigrants. Others receive training to teach English as a second language or to accompany people as they seek citizenship. Some even support new immigrant businesses or serve as guardians to unaccompanied minors.

WHAT KIND OF WORLD?

This book began with the notion that humans are storytelling animals and that migration is a compelling story. We found out along the way that the larger cultural narratives about migration do not always hold up well against the realities of migration or when compared to the teachings and ethics of human religious traditions like Christianity. We ended with a few ways for people of good will to put into practice their desire for a better and more just world. It should be obvious by now that what we decide to *do* about migration, either individually or as communities, depends a great deal on the narratives we trust not only regarding migration but also about the world itself, about our communities, even about God and ultimate meaning. For example, Christians look to Jesus, who during his lifetime wove together a narrative he called the reign or kingdom of God. It was a vision of the world turned upside down by God, where even those rejected in society had their rightful place, where forgiveness overcame vengeance, and where God's generous love would be the ultimate law.

A few years back, a student thanked me for soliciting contributions to an informal fund to help undocumented students apply for Deferred Action for Childhood Arrivals, or DACA, a protection against deportation that came with a work permit. Hours later, I wondered whether I

THEOLOGICAL NARRATIVES AND MIGRATION

deserved such thanks. Yes, I had wanted to help, but I also thought of it as an investment in the kind of country and world I wanted to live in, one that would have a place for young people like them. There is a joke Catholics used to tell on themselves. A woman finds her way to heaven and St. Peter obliges her with a tour. As they stroll around and see the magnificent sites, she suddenly glimpses an enormous wall at the end of a street. This seems incongruous to her—a giant wall in heaven. She asks St. Peter about it. "Oh," he says and smiles, "that's for some of the Catholics who think they are the only ones here." The joke slyly demands that we decide what kind of world we want to live in—a world just for people like me or a world for all of us.

NOTES

1. Migration in Recollection

1. See Daniel G. Groody, *Border of Death, Valley of Life: An Immigrant Journey of Heart and Spirit* (Lanham, MD: Rowman & Littlefield, 2002).

2. Paul Ricœur, "Narrative Identity," *Philosophy Today* 35, no. 1 (Spring 1991): 73.

3. R. Ruard Ganzevoort, "Introduction: Religious Stories We Live By," in *Religious Stories We Live By: Narrative Approaches in Theology and Religious Studies*, ed. Michael Scherer-Rath, Maaike de Haardt, and R. Ruard Ganzevoort (Leiden, Netherlands: Brill, 2014), 3.

4. Stephen Crites, "The Narrative Quality of Experience," *Journal of the American Academy of Religion* 39, no. 3 (September 1971): 305.

5. William C. Dowling, *Ricoeur on Time and Narrative: An Introduction to* Temps et Récit (Notre Dame, IN: University of Notre Dame Press, 2011), 37–52.

6. Dowling, *Ricoeur on Time and Narrative*, 48.

7. Hanna Meretoja, *The Ethics of Storytelling: Narrative Hermeneutics, History, and the Possible* (New York: Oxford University Press, 2018), 48.

8. Crites, "The Narrative Quality of Experience," 304.

9. Meretoja, *The Ethics of Storytelling*, 48–49.

10. Yuval Noah Harari, *Sapiens: A Brief History of Humankind* (New York: Harper Collins, 2015), 3–39; see also Peter Bellwood; *First Migrants: Ancient Migration in Global Perspective* (Malden, MA: Wiley Blackwell, 2013), 36–70.

11. Harari, *Sapiens*, 13–19.

12. See Rhacel Salazar Parreñas, "The Care Crisis in the Philippines: Children and Transnational Families in the New Global Economy," in *Global Woman: Nannies, Maids, and Sex Workers in the New Economy*, ed. Barbara Ehrenreich and Arlie Russell Hochschild (New York: Henry Holt, 2002), 39–54.

13. Michele Saracino, *Being about Borders: A Christian Anthropology of Difference* (Collegeville, MN: Liturgical Press, 2011), 23–24, 42–44.

14. The ethicist Tisha Rajendra warns specifically about the dangers of embracing "one true story" in accounts of migration. See Tisha M. Rajendra, *Migrants and Citizens: Justice and Responsibility in the Ethics of Immigration* (Grand Rapids, MI: Eerdmans, 2017), 128.

15. See, e.g., G.H. Bower, "Mood and Memory," *American Psychologist* 36 (1981): 129–48; Edward R. Hirt, Hugh E. McDonald, and Keith D. Markmann, "Expectancy Effects in Reconstructive Memory: When the Past Is Just What We Expected," in *Truth and Memory*, ed. Steven J. Lynn and Kevin M. McConkey (New York: Guilford Press, 1998), 62–89; Elizabeth Loftus, "The Reality of Illusory Memories," in *Memory Distortion*, ed. D. Schacter et al. (Cambridge, MA: Harvard University Press, 1995), 47–68; Elizabeth and Geoffrey Loftus, "On the Permanence of Stored Information in the Human Brain," *American Psychologist* 35, no. 5 (May 1980): 409–20; and J.M. Williams, F.N. Watts, C. MacLeod, and A. Mathews, *Cognitive Psychology and Emotional Disorders* (Chichester, UK: Wiley, 1997).

16. Brett C. Hoover, "Memory and Ministry: Young Adult Nostalgia, Immigrant Amnesia," *New Theology Review* 23, no. 1 (February 2010): 62–64.

17. Aristide R. Zolberg, *A Nation by Design: Immigration Policy in the Fashioning of America* (Cambridge, MA: Harvard University Press, 2006), 196.

18. Claude S. Fischer and Michael Hout, *A Century of Difference: How America Changed in the Last One Hundred Years* (New York: Russell Sage, 2006), 42–43.

19. Tara Bahrampour, "They Considered Themselves White, but DNA Tests Told a More Complex Story," *Washington Post*, February 6, 2018, https://www.washingtonpost.com/local/social-issues/they-considered-themselves-white-but-dna-tests-told-a-more-complex-story/2018/02/06/16215d1a-e181-11e7-8679-a9728984779c_story.html?noredirect=on&utm_term=.cf673d12b985.

20. Simon C. Kim, *Memory and Honor: Cultural and Generational Ministry with Korean American Communities* (Collegeville, MN: Liturgical Press, 2013), 44–64.

21. Rajendra, *Migrants and Citizens*, 127–28.

22. Svetlana Boym, *The Svetlana Boym Reader* (New York: Bloomsbury Academic, 2018), 233–55.

23. Robert Lasalle-Klein, *Blood and Ink: Ignacio Ellacuría, Jon Sobrino, and the Jesuit Martyrs of the University of Central America* (Maryknoll, NY: Orbis, 2014), 221.

24. Irene Nowell, Toni Craven, and Demitrius Dumm, "Tobit," in *The New Jerome Biblical Commentary*, ed. Raymond E. Brown, Joseph A. Fitzmyer, and Roland E. Murphy (Englewood Cliffs, NJ: Prentice Hall, 1990), 570.

2. Migration in Reality

1. United Nations, Department of Economic and Social Affairs, Population Division, "International Migration Report 2017" (New York: United Nations, 2017), x, 9; and Ronald Skeldon, "International Migration, Internal Migration, Mobility and Urbanization: Towards More Integrated Approaches," United Nations Expert Meeting Group on Sustainable Cities, Human Mobility, and International Migration, September 5, 2017, 3–4.

2. U.S. State Department Bureau of Western Hemisphere Affairs, Fact Sheet, April 1, 2018, https://www.state.gov/r/pa/ei/bgn/35749.htm.

3. The twenty nations are India, Mexico, Russia, China, Bangladesh, Syria, Pakistan, Ukraine, Philippines, United Kingdom, Afghanistan, Poland, Indonesia, Germany, Kazakhstan, Palestine, Romania, Turkey, Egypt, and Italy.

4. United States of America, Saudi Arabia, Germany, Russia, the United Kingdom, the United Arab Emirates, France, Canada, Australia, and Spain.

5. United Nations, "International Migration Report 2017," 1–38.

6. Alberto Alesina, Armando Miano, and Stefanie Stantcheva, "Immigration and Redistribution," Working Paper No. 24733, National Bureau of Economic Research, issued in June 2018, revised in October 2018.

7. Elizabeth M. Grieco, Edward Trevelyan, and Luke Larsen, et al., "The Size, Place of Birth, and Geographic Distribution of the Foreign-Born Population in the United States: 1960 to 2010," Working Paper no. 96 (Washington, DC: U.S. Census Bureau, October 2012), 3–6.

8. Grieco, Trevelyan, and Larsen, et al., "The Size, Place of Birth," 26–29.

9. See, e.g., Craig Childs, *Atlas of a Lost World: Travels in Ice Age America* (New York: Pantheon, 2018), on the debates about when human beings arrived in the Americas.

10. See, e.g., Paul E. Lovejoy, *Transformations in Slavery: A History of Slavery in Africa*, 3rd ed. (Cambridge: Cambridge University Press, 2012).

11. "Benjamin Franklin and the Pennsylvania Germans," in *American Nativism, 1830–1860*, ed. Ira M. Leonard and Robert D. Parmet (New York: Van Nostrand Reinhold Company, 1971), 115–16.

12. Brett C. Hoover, *The Shared Parish: Latinos, Anglos, and the Future of US Catholicism* (New York: NYU Press, 2014), 177.

13. Damany M. Fisher, *Discovering Early California Afro-Latino Presence* (Berkeley: Heyday Press, 2010), 3–24.

14. Ronald Takaki, *Strangers from a Different Shore: A History of Asian Americans* (New York: Penguin, 1989), 79–131; and Alexander Saxton, *The Indispensable Enemy: Labor and the Anti-Chinese Movement in California* (Berkeley: University of California, 1995).

15. Aristotle R. Zolberg, *A Nation by Design: Immigration Policy in the Fashioning of America* (New York: Russell Sage, 2007), 193–98.

16. Isabel Wilkerson, *The Warmth of Other Suns: The Epic Story of the Great Migration* (New York: Random House, 2010), 8–15, 37–46.

17. Zolberg, *A Nation by Design*, 80–87.

18. Zolberg, *A Nation by Design*, 99–165.

19. Zolberg, *A Nation by Design*, 166–68.

20. Zolberg, *A Nation by Design*, 166–98.

21. Zolberg, *A Nation by Design*, 258–64.

22. Alejandro Portes and Rubén Rumbaut, *Immigrant America: A Portrait*, 3rd ed. (Berkeley: University of California Press, 2006), 15–16.

23. Portes and Rumbaut, *Immigrant America*, 16; Frank D. Bean and Gillian Stevens, *America's Newcomers and the Dynamics of Diversity*, Rose Series in Sociology (New York: Russell Sage, 2003), 29–30.

24. Bean and Stevens, *America's Newcomers*, 30–31.

25. Bean and Stevens, *America's Newcomers*, 31–33.

26. Portes and Rumbaut, *Immigrant America*, 17.

27. Bean and Stevens, *America's Newcomers*, 33.

28. Portes and Rumbaut, *Immigrant America*, 20–34.

29. Portes and Rumbaut, *Immigrant America*, 92–93.

30. Portes and Rumbaut, *Immigrant America*, 25.

31. Portes and Rumbaut, *Immigrant America*, 30.

32. Claude S. Fischer and Michael Hout, *A Century of Difference: How America Changed in the Last One Hundred Years* (New York: Russell Sage, 2006), 43.

33. Samuel Huntington, *Who Are We? The Challenges to America's National Identity* (New York: Simon & Schuster, 2004), 221–56.

34. See, e.g., Louis Menand, "Patriot Games: The New Nativism of Samuel Huntington," *New Yorker*, May 17, 2004, https://www.newyorker.com/magazine/2004/05/17/patriot-games.

35. See, e.g., William B. Gudykunst, *Theorizing about Intercultural Communication* (Thousand Oaks, CA: SAGE Publications, 2005).

36. *Frank Leslie's Illustrated Newspaper* 54 (April 1, 1882): 96, located in Library of Congress Prints and Photographs Online Catalogue, http://loc.gov/pictures/resource/cph.3b48680/.

37. Hoover, *The Shared Parish*, 115.

38. "Assimilation," Online Etymology Dictionary, accessed January 21, 2019, https://www.etymonline.com/word/assimilate.

39. Robert Ezra Park and Ernest W. Burgess, *Introduction to the Science of Sociology* (Chicago: University of Chicago Press, 1921), 735, quoted in Richard Alba and Victor Nee, *Remaking the American Mainstream: Assimilation and Contemporary Immigration* (Cambridge, MA: Harvard University Press, 2003), 19.

40. Alba and Nee, *Remaking the American Mainstream*, 18–23; and Tomás R. Jiménez, *The Other Side of Assimilation: How Immigrants Are Changing American Life* (Berkeley: University of California Press, 2017), 6.

41. Alba and Nee, *Remaking the American Mainstream*, 23 27; and Jiménez, *The Other Side of Assimilation*, 6–7.

42. Jiménez, *The Other Side of Assimilation*, 7–8.

43. Jiménez, *The Other Side of Assimilation*, 8–9; and Alejandro Portes and Rubén Rumbaut, *Legacies: The Story of the Immigrant*

Second Generation (Berkeley: University of California Press, 2001), 46–49.

44. Portes and Rumbaut, *Legacies*, 59–62.

45. Tomás R. Jiménez, *Replenished Ethnicity: Mexican Americans, Immigration, and Identity* (Berkeley: University of California Press, 2010), 24.

46. Jiménez, *Replenished Ethnicity*, 21.

47. American Community Survey, 2013, U.S. Census Bureau.

48. Jiménez, *Replenished Ethnicity*, 20–24.

49. Interview with Marco Gutierrez, MSNBC, September 1, 2016, https://www.msnbc.com/all-in/watch/taco-trucks-on-every-corner-756382787934.

50. Jiménez, *The Other Side of Assimilation*, 11.

51. Peggy Levitt, *God Needs No Passport: Immigrants and the Changing American Religious Landscape* (New York: New Press, 2007), 37–46.

52. Levitt, *God Needs No Passport*, 53.

53. Kirk Semple, "Migrants' Emotional Ties to U.S. Expressed in Flags, Tombs and Fancy Homes," *New York Times*, September 9, 2018, https://www.nytimes.com/2018/09/09/world/americas/guatemala-migration.html.

II. CULTURAL NARRATIVES AND MIGRATION

1. Theodore Roosevelt, *A Most Glorious Ride: The Diaries of Theodore Roosevelt, 1877–1886*, ed. Edward P. Kohn (Albany: State University of New York Press, 2015), 214.

2. Karla Cornejo Villavicencio, *The Undocumented Americans* (New York: Random House, 2020), 4.

3. American Dreams and Nightmares

3. Perhaps the most impartial and comprehensive analysis of the economic and employment impact of immigrants on both low-wage and professional sectors is from the National Academies of Sciences, Engineering, and Medicine, *The Economic and Fiscal Consequences of Immigration* (Washington, DC: The National Academies Press, 2017), 197–278.

4. Ched Myers, "Our God Is Undocumented: Sanctuary and Prophetic Hospitality," in *Our God Is Undocumented: Biblical Faith and Immigrant Justice*, ed. Ched Myers and Matthew Collwell (Maryknoll, NY: Orbis Books, 2012), 64.

5. Julian Brookes, "Oscars: How *A Better Life*'s Chris Weitz and Demian Bichir Got Political," *Rolling Stone*, February 24, 2012, https://www.rollingstone.com/politics/politics-news/oscars-how-a-better-lifes-chris-weitz-and-demian-bichir-got-political-188524/.

6. William A.V. Clark, *Immigration and the American Dream: Remaking the Middle Class* (New York: Guilford Press, 2003), 3–4.

7. Clark, *Immigration and the American Dream*, 6–9. See also Sandra L. Hanson and John Kenneth White, eds., introduction to *The American Dream in the 21st Century* (Philadelphia: Temple University Press, 2011), 9.

8. Hanson and White, introduction to *The American Dream*, 1–2.

9. Luke Winslow, *Economic Injustice and the Rhetoric of the American Dream* (New York: Lexington Books, 2017), 22–27.

10. Clark, *Immigration and the American Dream*, 4.

11. Clark, *Immigration and the American Dream*, 4.

12. Ambar Narayan et al., *Fair Progress? Economic Mobility across Generations around the World* (Washington, DC: International Bank for Reconstruction and Development / The World Bank, 2018), 127.

13. George J. Borjas, "Making It in America: Social Mobility in the Immigrant Population," *The Future of Children* 16, no. 2 (Autumn 2006): 57.

14. Alejandro Portes and Rubén Rumbaut, *Legacies: The Story of the Immigrant Second Generation* (Berkeley: University of California Press, 2001), 72–85.

15. Frank D. Bean and Gillian Stevens, *America's Newcomers and the Dynamics of Diversity*, Rose Series in Sociology (New York: Russell Sage, 2003), 140.

16. Stephanie Coontz, *The Way We Never Were: American Families and the Nostalgia Trip* (New York: Basic Books, 2000), 24.

17. Coontz, *The Way We Never Were*, 24, 77.

18. It is also worth noting that the government assistance associated with the postwar period—the G.I. Bill and other forms of higher education support, government guarantees on housing loans,

infrastructure building—disproportionately benefited whites and, in some cases, were simply unavailable to African Americans in any meaningful way because of discriminatory housing and education practices. See Mary Ann Lamanna and Agnes Riedmann, *Marriage, Families, and Relationships: Making Choices in a Diverse Society*, 11th ed. (Belmont, CA: Wadsworth Cengage Learning, 2012), 52.

19. Carl Bon Tempo, "Refugees, Asylees, and Immigrants," in *Immigrants in American History: Arrival, Adaptation, and Integration*, ed. Elliott Robert Barkan (Santa Barbara: ABC-CLIO, 2013), 1521.

20. Bon Tempo, "Refugees, Asylees, and Immigrants," 1521–37.

21. "Trump Says Mexico Sending 'Rapists' across Border," *Fox News*, June 16, 2015, https://www.foxnews.com/politics/trump -says-mexico-sending-rapists-across-border-hed-make-country-pay-for -border-wall.

22. Mark Krikorian, "America, the Dumping Ground," *National Review*, December 9, 2016, https://www.nationalreview.com/corner/ dumping-other-countries-refugee-problems-america/.

23. Michael T. Light and Ty Miller, "Does Undocumented Immigration Increase Violent Crime?," *Criminology* 56, no. 2 (May 2018): 370–401.

24. "Remarks by President Trump at a California Sanctuary State Roundtable," transcript from the White House, May 16, 2018, https:// www.whitehouse.gov/briefings-statements/remarks-president-trump -california-sanctuary-state-roundtable/.

25. Emily M. Farris and Heather Silber Mohamed, "Picturing Immigration: How the Media Criminalizes Immigrants," *Politics, Groups, and Identities* 6, no. 4 (2018): 814–24, https://doi.org/10.1080/ 21565503.2018.1484375.

26. Thomas R. Whitney, *A Defence of the American Policy, as Opposed to the Encroachments of Foreign Influence, and Especially to the Interference of the Papacy in the Political Interests and Affairs of the United States* (New York: De Witt & Davenport, 1856), 236, Making of America digital library, University of Michigan, 2005, https://quod .lib.umich.edu/m/moa/ahm4910.0001.001/236?rgn=full+text;view= image;q1=Irish.

27. Carolyn Moehling and Anne Morrison Piehl, "Immigration, Crime, and Incarceration in Early Twentieth-Century America," *Demography* 46, no. 4 (2009): 739–63.

28. Charles Kurzman, *Muslim-American Involvement with Violent Extremism, 2001–2018* (Durham, NC: Duke University Triangle Center on Terrorism and Homeland Security, 2019), 2–3.

29. Center on Extremism of the Anti-Defamation League, *Murder and Extremism in the United States in 2018* (New York: Anti-Defamation League, 2019), 4.

30. Kurzman, *Muslim-American Involvement*, 6.

31. Leo Chavez, *The Latino Threat: Constructing Immigrants, Citizens, and the Nation* (Stanford, CA: Stanford University Press, 2008), 2.

32. Robert Adelman, Lesley Williams Reid, Gail Markle, Saskia Weiss, and Charles Jaret, "Urban Crime Rates and the Changing Face of Immigration: Evidence across Four Decades," *Journal of Ethnicity in Criminal Justice* 15, no. 1 (2017): 52–77, https://doi.org/10.1080/15377938.2016.1261057. See also Graham C. Ousey and Charis E. Kubrin's comprehensive assessment of research refuting a link between immigration and crime, "Immigration and Crime: Assessing a Contentious Issue," *Annual Review of Criminology* 1, no. 1 (2018): 63–84.

33. Alex Nowrasteh, "Illegal Immigrants and Crime—Assessing the Evidence," Cato Institute, accessed April 11, 2019, https://www.cato.org/blog/illegal-immigrants-crime-assessing-evidence.

34. Richard Alba and Victor Nee, *Remaking the American Mainstream: Assimilation and Contemporary Immigration* (Cambridge, MA: Harvard University Press, 2003), 217–30.

35. Alejandro Portes and Rubén Rumbaut, *Immigrant America: A Portrait*, 3rd ed. (Berkeley: University of California Press, 2006), 212–18.

36. Alba and Nee, *Remaking the American Mainstream*, 262.

37. Renee Stepler and Mark Hugo Lopez, "U.S. Latino Population Growth and Dispersion Has Slowed since Onset of the Great Recession," Pew Research Center, September 8, 2016, https://www.pewhispanic.org/2016/09/08/latino-population-growth-and-dispersion-has-slowed-since-the-onset-of-the-great-recession/.

38. Chavez, *The Latino Threat*, 78–87.

39. Chavez, *The Latino Threat*, 88–90.

40. Chavez, *The Latino Threat*, 21–43, cartoon, 35.

41. Chavez, *The Latino Threat*, 3.

42. Lee Bebout, *Whiteness on the Border: Mapping the U.S. Racial Imagination in Brown and White* (New York: NYU Press, 2016), 3.

43. Brett C. Hoover, *The Shared Parish: Latinos, Anglos, and the Future of U.S. Catholicism* (New York: NYU Press, 2014), 77–78.

44. Nowrasteh, "Illegal Immigrants and Crime."

45. Jeffrey S. Passel and D'Vera Cohn, "U.S. Unauthorized Immigrant Total Dips to Lowest Level in a Decade," Pew Research Center, November 27, 2018 (Washington, DC: Pew Research Center, 2018), 5–7.

46. Passel and Cohn, "U.S. Unauthorized Immigrant Total Dips to Lowest Level in a Decade," 22–26.

47. Brett C. Hoover, "Blaming the Stranger," *America* 214, no. 17 (May 16, 2016): 24.

48. Bebout, *Whiteness on the Border*, 33–72.

49. Bebout, *Whiteness on the Border*, 63–64, 71–72.

50. Efrén O. Pérez, "Explicit Evidence on the Import of Implicit Attitudes: The IAT and Immigration Policy Judgments," *Political Behavior* 32, no. 4 (December 2010): 517–45.

51. Robert Warren, "US Undocumented Population Continued to Fall from 2016 to 2017, and Visa Overstays Significantly Exceeded Illegal Crossings for the Seventh Consecutive Year," Center for Migration Studies of New York, January 16, 2019, https://cmsny.org/publications/essay-2017-undocumented-and-overstays/.

52. Gemma Tulud Cruz, *Toward a Theology of Migration: Social Justice and Religious Experience* (New York: Palgrave McMillan, 2014), 17.

53. Tisha M. Rajendra, *Migrants and Citizens: Justice and Responsibility in the Ethics of Immigration* (Grand Rapids, MI: Eerdmans, 2017), 128.

4. Longing and Loss

1. Karla Cornejo Villavicencio, *The Undocumented Americans* (New York: Random House, 2020), 4.

2. Patrick J. McDonnell, "To Folks in This Guatemalan Town, Success Stories Start with a Trek to the U.S.," *Los Angeles Times*, July 21, 2019, https://www.latimes.com/world/mexico-americas/la-fg-migrants-todossantos-20190711-story.html.

3. Isabel Wilkerson, *The Warmth of Other Suns: The Epic Story of the Great Migration* (New York: Random House, 2010), 172–73.

4. Daniel E. Martínez, Jeremy Slack, Alex E. Chávez, and Scott Whiteford, "'The American Dream': Walking Toward and Deporting

It," in *The Latino/a American Dream,* ed. Sandra L. Hanson and John Kenneth White (College Station: Texas A&M University Press, 2016), 91–92.

5. Martínez et al., "American Dream," 82.

6. Gurcharn S. Basran and Li Zong, "Devaluation of Foreign Credentials as Perceived by Visible Minority Professional Immigrants," *Canadian Ethnic Studies Journal* 30, no. 3 (Fall 1998): 8.

7. Daniel G. Groody, *Border of Death, Valley of Life: An Immigrant Journey of Heart and Spirit* (Lanham, MD: Rowman & Littlefield, 2002), 24–25.

8. Brett C. Hoover, *The Shared Parish: Latinos, Anglos, and the Future of U.S. Catholicism* (New York: NYU Press, 2014), 93–94.

9. Groody, *Border of Death, Valley of Life,* 26–33.

10. Hoover, *The Shared Parish,* 93–99.

11. Martínez et al., "American Dream," 81–82.

12. Martínez et al., "American Dream," 94.

13. Simon C. Kim, *Memory and Honor: Cultural and Generational Ministry with Korean American Communities* (Collegeville, MN: Liturgical Press, 2013), 56–64.

14. This dynamic is poignantly demonstrated in Elaine Castillo's novel of Filipino immigrant families, *America Is Not the Heart* (New York: Viking, 2018).

15. Alejandro Portes and Rubén Rumbaut, *Immigrant America: A Portrait,* 3rd ed. (Berkeley: University of California Press, 2006), 263–67.

16. Wilkerson, *The Warmth of Other Suns,* 39.

17. Sarah Stillman, "When Deportation Is a Death Sentence," *New Yorker,* January 15, 2018, https://www.newyorker.com/magazine/2018/01/15/when-deportation-is-a-death-sentence?irclickid=0U9yTXWyExyJRcqwUx0Mo34VUklWqHyvFSTzV80&irgwc=1&source=affiliate_impactpmx_12f6tote_desktop_Viglink%20Primary&utm_source=impact-affiliate&utm_medium=27795&utm_campaign=impact&utm_content=Online%20Tracking%20Link&utm_brand=tny.

18. Jonathan Blitzer, "The Teens Trapped between a Gang and the Law," *New Yorker,* January 1, 2018, https://www.newyorker.com/magazine/2018/01/01/the-teens-trapped-between-a-gang-and-the-law.

19. Campbell Gibson and Kay Jung, "Historical Census Statistics on the Foreign-Born Population of the United States: 1850–2000," Population Division Working Paper no. 81 (Washington, DC: U.S. Census Bureau, 2006), table 3.

20. Jonathan Blitzer, "The Dream Homes of Guatemalan Migrants," *New Yorker*, April 5, 2019, https://www.newyorker.com/news/dispatch/the-dream-homes-of-guatemalan-migrants.

21. Esther Pérez Ruiz, "Impact of Remittances on Household Decisions in Guatemala," *Diálogo a Fondo*, International Monetary Fund, August 14, 2018, https://www.imf.org/external/np/blog/dialogo/081418.pdf.

22. McDonnell, "To Folks in This Guatemalan Town."

5. Migration as Holy History

1. John Thompson, "Seeking the 'Farther Shore': Buddhism as Spiritual Immigration," in *Strangers in This World: Multireligious Reflections on Immigration*, ed. Hussam S. Timani, Allen G. Jorgenson, and Alexander Y. Hwang (Minneapolis: Fortress Press, 2015), 31–50.

2. Hussam S. Timani, "The Islamic Doctrine of *Hijra* (Migration)," in *Strangers in this World*, 115–17.

3. Amir Hussain, "Toward a Muslim Theology of Migration," in *Theology of Migration in the Abrahamic Traditions*, ed. Elaine Padilla and Peter Phan (New York: Palgrave MacMillan, 2014), 174–79.

4. Zeynab Sayilgan, "Islamic Creation Theology and the Human Being as Migrant," in *The Meaning of My Neighbor's Faith: Interreligious Reflections on Immigration*, ed. Alexander Y. Hwang and Laura E. Alexander (Lanham, MD: Academic Press, 2018), 8–11.

5. Sayilgan, "Islamic Creation Theology," 5–8.

6. Muhammad Shafiq, "Immigration Theology in Islam," in *Strangers in this World*, 97–109.

6. Biblical Narratives of Migration

1. Donald Senior, *What Are They Saying About Matthew?*, rev. ed. (New York: Paulist Press, 1996), 77–80.

2. See, e.g., David Cortés-Fuentes, "The Least of These My Brothers: Matthew 25:31–46," *Apuntes* 23, no. 3 (Fall 2003): 107–9.

3. See, e.g., Emily McFarlan Miller and Yonat Shimron, "Why Is Jeff Sessions Quoting Romans 13 and Why Is the Bible Verse So Often Invoked?," *USA Today*, June 16, 2018, https://www.usatoday.com/story/news/2018/06/16/jeff-sessions-bible-romans-13-trump-immigration-policy/707749002/; and Lincoln Mullen; "The Fight

to Define Romans 13," *The Atlantic*, June 15, 2018, https://www
.theatlantic.com/ideas/archive/2018/06/romans-13/562916/.

4. Raymond Brown, *An Introduction to the New Testament* (New Haven, CT: Yale University Press, 1997), 559–64, 571–72.

5. Peter C. Phan, "Migration in the Patristic Era: History and Theology," in *A Promised Land, a Perilous Journey: Theological Perspectives on Migration*, ed. Daniel G. Groody and Gioacchino Campese (Notre Dame, IN: University of Notre Dame Press, 2008), 37–38.

6. See M. Daniel Carroll R., *Christians at the Border: Immigration, the Church, and the Bible*, 2nd ed. (Grand Rapids, MI: Brazos Press, 2013), 53–56.

7. See Letty M. Russell, *Just Hospitality: God's Welcome in a World of Difference* (Louisville, KY: Westminster John Knox, 2009), 82–83.

8. Markus Zehnder, "Mass Migration to the Western World in Light of the Hebrew Bible: The Challenge of Complexity," *European Journal of Theology* 27, no. 1 (2018): 5–8 [4–17].

9. Zehnder, "Mass Migration," 5. It must be said that identification of the *gerim* as strangers or immigrants is not without controversy in Jewish and Christian circles. See, e.g., Stuart Krauss, "The Word *Ger* in the Bible and Its Implications," *Jewish Bible Quarterly* 34, no. 4 (2006): 264–70; and Mark Glanville, "The Gēr (Stranger) in Deuteronomy: Family for the Displaced," *Journal of Biblical Literature* 137, no. 3 (2018): 599–623. By the rabbinical era, there was widespread use of the term *gerim* mainly to describe Jewish converts.

10. See, e.g., Ched Myers, "Our God Is Undocumented: Sanctuary and Prophetic Hospitality," in *Our God Is Undocumented: Biblical Faith and Immigrant Justice* (Maryknoll, NY: Orbis, 2012), 53–71.

11. Anne-Mareike Schol-Wetter, "A Nomadic Approach to the Hebrew Bible," in *The Bible and Feminism: Remapping the Field*, ed. Yvonne Sherwood (New York: Oxford University Press, 2017), 339.

12. Hannah Hartig, "Republicans Turn More Negative toward Refugees as Number Admitted to U.S. Plummets," *Pew Research Center Fact Tank*, May 24, 2018, https://www.pewresearch.org/fact-tank/2018/05/24/republicans-turn-more-negative-toward-refugees-as-number-admitted-to-u-s-plummets/.

13. Donald Senior, "'Beloved Aliens and Exiles': New Testament Perspectives on Migration," in *A Promised Land, A Perilous Journey: Theological Perspectives on Migration*, ed. Daniel G. Groody and

Gioacchino Campese (Notre Dame, IN: University of Notre Dame Press, 2009), 20–29.

14. Senior, "Beloved Aliens and Exiles," 30.

15. Senior, "Beloved Aliens and Exiles," 32.

16. James K. Hoffmeier, *The Immigration Crisis: Immigrants, Aliens, and the Bible* (Wheaton, IL: Crossway, 2009), 141–44.

17. Hoffmeier, *The Immigration Crisis*, 48–52, 71–96.

18. Hoffmeier, *The Immigration Crisis*, 29–57.

19. Manlio Granziano, *What Is a Border?* (Stanford, CA: Stanford University Press, 2018), 13–14.

20. Carroll, *Christians at the Border*, 45–51.

21. Carroll, *Christians at the Border*, 71.

22. Carroll, *Christians at the Border*, 75–101.

23. Carroll, *Christians at the Border*, 106–16.

24. Carroll, *Christians at the Border*, 127.

25. Carroll, *Christians at the Border*, 122–27.

26. Ched Myers, *Binding the Strong Man: A Political Reading of Mark's Story of Jesus*, ann. ed. (Maryknoll, NY: Orbis Books, 2008).

27. Myers, "Our God Is Undocumented," 57.

28. Myers, "Our God Is Undocumented," 53–61.

29. Myers, "Our God Is Undocumented," 65.

30. Myers, "Our God Is Undocumented," 61–71.

IV. THEOLOGICAL NARRATIVES AND MIGRATION

1. *Saint Benedict's Rule for Monasteries*, trans. Leonard J. Doyle, OblSB (Collegeville, MN: Liturgical Press, 1948, 2001), http://archive.osb.org/rb/text/rbeaad1.html#53.

7. Migration in Christian History and Tradition

2. Lucretia Yaghjian, *Writing Theology Well: A Rhetoric for Theological and Biblical Writers* (New York: Bloomsbury T&T Clark, 2015), 102.

3. Peter C. Phan, "Migration in the Patristic Era: History and Theology," in *A Promised Land, a Perilous Journey: Theological Perspectives on Migration*, ed. Daniel G. Groody and Gioacchino Campese (Notre Dame, IN: University of Notre Dame Press, 2008), 35–36.

4. Samuel N.C. Lieu and Ken Parry, "Deep into Asia," in *Early Christianity in Context: An Exploration across Cultures and Continents*, ed. William Tabbernee (Grand Rapids, MI: Baker Academic, 2014), 159–66.

5. See, e.g., Susan E. Hylen, *A Modest Apostle: Thecla and the History of Women in the Early Church* (New York: Oxford University Press, 2015), 92–98.

6. Hylen, *A Modest Apostle*, 38–40.

7. See Cornelia Horn, Samuel N. C. Lieu, and Robert R. Phenix Jr., "Beyond the Eastern Frontier"; Christopher Haas, "The Caucasus"; and Samuel N. C. Lieu and Ken Parry, "Deep into Asia," in Tabbernee, *Early Christianity in Context*, 111–80.

8. Phan, "Migration in the Patristic Era," 41–47.

9. "The Didache of the Twelve Apostles," trans. Aelred Cody, OSB, in *The Didache in Context: Essays on Its Text, History and Transmission*, ed. Clayton N. Jefford (Leiden: Brill, 1995), 3–14.

10. "Epistle to Diognetus" 5.5, in *The Epistle to Diognetus: Introduction, Text, and Commentary*, ed. Clayton Jefford (New York: Oxford University Press, 2013), 145.

11. Basil, "Letter 94," in *And You Welcomed Me: A Sourcebook on Hospitality in Early Christianity*, ed. Amy G. Oden (Nashville: Abingdon Press, 2001), 218.

12. Phan, "Migration in the Patristic Era," 49–54.

13. Diarmaid MacCulloch, *Christianity: The First Three Thousand Years* (New York: Penguin, 2009), 436–42.

14. MacCulloch, *Christianity*, 367–68.

15. Thomas Merton, *Mystics and Zen Masters* (New York: Farrar, Straus, and Giroux, 1961), 95–98.

16. Lateran IV, canon 9, Medieval Sourcebook, Fordham University, accessed November 17, 2020, https://sourcebooks.fordham.edu/basis/lateran4.asp.

17. Manlio Granziano, *What Is a Border?* (Stanford, CA: Stanford University Press, 2018), 14–21.

18. Becky Taylor, *Another Darkness, Another Dawn: A History of Gypsies, Roma, and Travellers* (London: Reaktion Books, 2014), 37–64.

19. See, e.g., Marie Therese Archambault, Mark G. Thiel, and Christopher Vecsey, eds., *The Crossing of Two Roads: Being Catholic and Native in the United States* (Maryknoll, NY: Orbis Books, 2003), 1–19, 54–60, 75–87.

20. See appendix to Bartolomé de las Casas, *De regia potestate o derecho de autodeterminación*, ed. Luciano Pereña et al., in *Corpus Hispanorum de Pace*, vol. 8 (Madrid: Consejo Superior de Investigaciones Científicas, 1969), 282–83, quoted in Luis N. Rivera-Pagán, "A Prophetic Challenge to the Church: The Last Word of Bartolomé de las Casas," inaugural lecture of Henry Winters Luce Professorship in Ecumenics and Mission, April 9, 2003, Princeton Theological Seminary.

21. Rainer Grote, "The Status and Rights of Indigenous Peoples in Latin America," *Zeitschrift für ausländisches öffentliches Recht und Völkerrecht / Heidelberg Journal of International Law* 59 (1999): 503–5.

22. Graziano, *What Is a Border?*, 19.

23. Peter Berger, Grace Davie, and Effie Fokas, *Religious America, Secular Europe?* (Burlington, VT: Ashgate, 2008), 27.

24. Charles E. Curran, *Catholic Social Teaching: A Historical, Theological, and Ethical Analysis* (Washington, DC: Georgetown University Press, 2002), 2–9; and Donal Dorr, *Option for the Poor: A Hundred Years of Vatican Social Teaching* (Maryknoll, NY: Orbis Books, 1983), 11–28.

25. Pius XII, apostolic constitution *Exsul Familia Nazarethana*, 1952, accessed November 17, 2020, https://www.papalencyclicals.net/pius12/p12exsul.htm; Archbishop José H. Gomez, *Immigration and the Next America: Renewing the Soul of Our Nation* (Huntington, IN: Our Sunday Visitor, 2013), 85–89; and Ezio Marchetto, *The Catholic Church and the Phenomenon of Migration: An Overview*, Center for Migration Studies Occasional Papers 10 (New York: Center for Migration Studies, 1989), 10–13.

26. John XXIII, *Pacem in Terris*, April 11, 1963, http://w2.vatican.va/content/john-xxiii/en/encyclicals/documents/hf_j-xxiii_enc_11041963_pacem.html; and Marchetto, *The Catholic Church*, 13–14.

27. Marchetto, *The Catholic Church*, 14–15.

28. Marchetto, *The Catholic Church*, 15.

29. Marchetto, *The Catholic Church*, 16–20; Gomez, *Immigration and the Next America*, 91; Jorge E. Castillo Guerra, "Contributions of the Social Teaching of the Roman Catholic Church on Migration:

From a 'Culture of Rejection' to a 'Culture of Encounter,'" *Exchange* 44 (2015): 419–22.

30. Castillo Guerra, "Contributions of the Social Teaching," 422–23.

31. United States Conference of Catholic Bishops and Conferencia del Episcopado Mexicano, "Strangers No Longer: Together on the Journey of Hope," 2003, nos. 33–38, http://www.usccb.org/issues-and-action/human-life-and-dignity/immigration/strangers-no-longer-together-on-the-journey-of-hope.cfm.

32. Castillo Guerra, "Contributions of Social Thought," 422–24.

33. Translation from the Spanish by the author.

8. Migration in Christian Ethics

1. Christian Scharen, *Faith as a Way of Life: A Vision for Pastoral Leadership* (Grand Rapids, MI: Eerdmans, 2008), 14–26.

2. See Graziano Battistella, "Migration and Human Dignity," in *A Promised Land, a Perilous Journey: Theological Perspectives on Migration*, ed. Daniel G. Groody and Gioacchino Campese (Notre Dame, IN: University of Notre Dame Press, 2008), 186–87; and Gemma Tulud Cruz, *Toward a Theology of Migration: Social Justice and Religious Experience* (New York: Palgrave MacMillan, 2014), 55–56.

3. Luke Bretherton, "The Duty of Care to Refugees, Christian Cosmopolitanism, and the Hallowing of Bare Life," *Studies in Christian Ethics* 19, no. 1 (2006): 49.

4. Carlos M.N. Eire, *Reformations: The Early Modern World, 1450–1650* (New Haven, CT: Yale University Press, 2016), 199–210. See also Mark M. Anschutz, *Just Immigration: American Policy in Christian Perspective* (Grand Rapids, MI: Eerdmans, 2017), 73–76, 127–39.

5. Anschutz, *Just Immigration*, 127.

6. Justin P. Ashworth, "Who Are Our People? Toward a Christian Witness against Borders," *Modern Theology* 34, no. 4 (October 2018): 500.

7. Ashworth, "Who Are Our People?," 500n23.

8. Nigel Biggar, *Between Kin and Cosmopolis: An Ethic of the Nation* (Eugene, OR: Cascade Books, 2014), 17.

9. Biggar, *Between Kin and Cosmopolis*, 17.

10. See, e.g., Bretherton, "The Duty of Care," 39–61.

11. Ashworth, "Who Are Our People?," 505–17.

12. Tisha M. Rajendra, *Migrants and Citizens: Justice and Responsibility in the Ethics of Immigration* (Grand Rapids, MI: Eerdmans, 2017), 13.

13. Bretherton, "The Duty of Care," 47.

14. Bretherton, "The Duty of Care," 43–50.

15. Miguel A. De la Torre, *Trails of Terror and Hope: Testimonies on Immigration* (Maryknoll, NY: Orbis Books, 2009), 131.

16. De la Torre, *Trails of Terror and Hope*, 132.

17. William O'Neill, "The Place of Displacement: The Ethics of Migration in the United States," in *Living with(out) Borders: Catholic Theological Ethics on the Migrations of Peoples*, ed. Agnes M. Brazal and María Teresa Dávila (Maryknoll, NY: Orbis Books, 2016), 68.

18. O'Neill, "The Place of Displacement," 69.

19. O'Neill, "The Place of Displacement," 72.

20. O'Neill, "The Place of Displacement," 72.

21. Kristin E. Heyer, *Kinship across Borders: A Christian Ethic of Immigration* (Washington, DC: Georgetown University Press, 2012), 18.

22. Heyer, *Kinship across Borders*, 11.

23. Heyer, *Kinship across Borders*, 10–14.

24. Heyer, *Kinship across Borders*, 17.

25. Heyer, *Kinship across Borders*, 14–27.

26. Heyer, *Kinship across Borders*, 46.

27. See, e.g., Valeria Luiselli, *Tell Me How It Ends: An Essay in Forty Questions* (Minneapolis: Coffee House Press, 2017); or Kristin Heyer, "Toward a Moral Response to Unaccompanied Minors in the US Context," and Tisha Rajendra, "Justice as Responsibility to Child Migrants," in *Unaccompanied Migrant Children: Social, Legal, and Ethical Perspectives*, ed. Hille Haker and Molly Greening (Lanham, MD: Lexington Books, 2019), 161–200.

28. Heyer, *Kinship across Borders*, 67.

29. Heyer, *Kinship across Borders*, 70.

30. Heyer, *Kinship across Borders*, 74–78.

31. Heyer, *Kinship across Borders*, 74–78.

32. Heyer, *Kinship across Borders*, 78–80.

33. Rajendra, *Migrants and Citizens*, 120–24; Heyer, *Kinship across Borders*, 78–87.

34. Rajendra, *Migrants and Citizens*, 125–26.

35. Rajendra, *Migrants and Citizens*, 120.

36. Rajendra, *Migrants and Citizens*, 130–33.

37. Marcelo Castillo and Skyler Simnitt, "Farm Labor," 2014–2016 data, U.S. Department of Agriculture, January 2020, https://www.ers.usda.gov/topics/farm-economy/farm-labor/.

38. Miriam Jordan, "Farmworkers, Mostly Undocumented, Become 'Essential' During Pandemic," *New York Times*, April 3, 2020, https://www.nytimes.com/2020/04/02/us/coronavirus-undocumented-immigrant-farmworkers-agriculture.html.

39. Jordan, "Farmworkers," 130–33.

9. Migration in Theology

1. Lizbeth de la Santa Cruz Santana, "Mural Project," accessed November 18, 2020, https://lizbethdelacruzsantana.com/mural-project.

2. Leanna Garfield, "A Mexican Artist Is Painting the 'World's Longest Mural' on the US–Mexico Border Wall," *Business Insider*, January 7, 2018, https://www.businessinsider.com/mexican-artist-enrique-chiu-border-wall-murals-2018-1.

3. Catherine LaCugna, *God for Us: The Trinity and Christian Life* (New York: HarperCollins, 1991), 6.

4. Peter C. Phan, "Deus Migrator—God the Migrant: Migration of Theology and Theology of Migration," *Theological Studies* 77, no. 4 (2016): 864.

5. Phan, "Deus Migrator," 855–66.

6. Phan, "Deus Migrator," 861.

7. Phan, "Deus Migrator," 861.

8. Daniel G. Groody, *Border of Death, Valley of Life: An Immigrant Journey of Heart and Spirit* (Lanham, MD: Rowman & Littlefield, 2002), 29.

9. Groody, *Border of Death*, 32–33.

10. Groody, *Border of Death*, 41–136.

11. Jon Sobrino, *The Principle of Mercy: Taking the Crucified People Down from the Cross* (Maryknoll, NY: Orbis Books, 1994); and Gioacchino Campese, "¿Cuántos Más? The Crucified Peoples at the U.S.–Mexico Border," in *A Promised Land, a Perilous Journey: Theological Perspectives on Migration*, ed. Daniel G. Groody and Gioacchino Campese (Notre Dame, IN: University of Notre Dame Press, 2008), 282–86.

12. U.S. Border Patrol, Southwest Border Deaths by Fiscal Year, accessed November 19, 2020, https://www.cbp.gov/sites/default/files/assets/documents/2019-Mar/bp-southwest-border-sector-deaths-fy1998-fy2018.pdf.

13. Campese, "¿Cuántos Más?," 291.

14. Nancy Pineda-Madrid, *Suffering and Salvation in Ciudad Juarez* (Nashville: Augsburg Fortress Publishers, 2011), 146.

15. Olivia Ruiz Marrujo, "The Gender of Risk: Sexual Violence against Undocumented Women," in Groody and Campese, eds., *A Promised Land, a Perilous Journey*, 225–39.

16. Nancy Pineda-Madrid, "Sex Trafficking and Feminicide at the Border: Re-Membering Our Daughters," in *Living with(out) Borders: Catholic Theological Ethics on the Migrations of Peoples*, ed. Agnes M. Brazal and María Teresa Dávila (Maryknoll, NY: Orbis Books, 2016), 88.

17. Pineda-Madrid, *Suffering and Salvation*, 124.

18. Carmen Nanko-Fernández, *Theologizing en Espanglish* (Maryknoll, NY: Orbis Books, 2010), 117.

19. Daniel G. Groody, "Cup of Suffering, Chalice of Salvation: Refugee, Lampedusa, and the Eucharist," *Theological Studies* 78, no. 4 (December 2017): 960–87, at 976.

20. See, e.g., James Cone, *The Cross and the Lynching Tree* (Maryknoll, NY: Orbis Books, 2013); or M. Shawn Copeland, *Enfleshing Freedom: Body, Race, and Being* (Nashville: Fortress Press, 2009).

21. Christine D. Pohl, *Making Room: Recovering Hospitality as a Christian Tradition* (Grand Rapids, MI: Eerdmans, 1999), 18.

22. Ana Maria Pineda, "Hospitality," in *Practicing Our Faith: A Way of Life for a Searching People*, ed. Dorothy C. Bass, 2nd ed. (San Francisco: Jossey-Bass, 2010), 32–34.

23. Pineda, "Hospitality," 29–31, 42.

24. Pineda, "Hospitality," 31.

25. Joshua W. Jipp, *Saved by Faith and Hospitality* (Grand Rapids, MI: Eerdmans, 2017), 12.

26. Jipp, *Saved by Faith and Hospitality*, 143.

27. Jipp, *Saved by Faith and Hospitality*, 142–46.

28. Nanko-Fernández, *Theologizing en Espanglish*, 116, 119.

29. Nell Becker Sweeden, *Church on the Way: Hospitality and Migration* (Eugene, OR: Pickwick Publications, 2015), 73.

30. Sweeden, *Church on the Way*, 73–76.

31. Sweeden, *Church on the Way*, 75.
32. Sweeden, *Church on the Way*, 74–79.
33. Sweeden, *Church on the Way*, 79.
34. Cruz, *Toward a Theology of Migration*, 95.
35. Cruz, *Toward a Theology of Migration*, 96.
36. Sweeden, *Church on the Way*, 79–89.

10. Conclusion

1. See, e.g., Ada María Isasi-Díaz, "*Lo Cotidiano*: A Key Element of Mujerista Theology," *Journal of Hispanic/Latino Theology* 10, no. 1 (2002): 5–17.

2. On the dangers of "one true story," see Michele Saracino, *Being about Borders: A Christian Anthropology of Difference* (Collegeville, MN: Liturgical Press, 2011), 23–24, 42–44; and Tisha M. Rajendra, *Migrants and Citizens: Justice and Responsibility in the Ethics of Immigration* (Grand Rapids, MI: Eerdmans, 2017), 128.

3. This is borne out in sociological research. See Tomás Jiménez, *The Other Side of Assimilation: How Immigrants Are Changing American Life* (Berkeley: University of California Press, 2017).

4. Pope Francis, Homily at the Cathedral of San Sebastian, Rio de Janeiro, Brazil, Saturday, July 27, 2013, http://www.vatican.va/content/francesco/en/homilies/2013/documents/papa-francesco_20130727_gmg-omelia-rio-clero.html.

5. Darren E. Sherkat and Derek Lehman, "Bad Samaritans: Religion and Anti-Immigrant and Anti-Muslim Sentiment in the United States," *Social Science Quarterly* 99, no. 5 (November 2018): 1793.

6. See Donald Kerwin, Daniela Alulema, Michael Nicholson, and Robert Warren, "Statelessness in the United States: A Study to Estimate and Profile the US Stateless Population," *Journal on Migration and Human Security* 8 (2020): 1–64, https://journals.sagepub.com/doi/pdf/10.1177/2331502420907028.

7. See Seth Freed Wessler, "Fear, Illness and Death in ICE Detention: How a Protest Grew on the Inside," *New York Times*, June 4, 2010, https://www.nytimes.com/2020/06/04/magazine/covid-ice.html.

INDEX